PENGUIN
ARKANA

# THE BOOK OF MIRDAD

Mikhail Naimy was born in 1889 in the Lebanese village of Biskinta which sits high on the slope of Mt. Sannin overlooking the Eastern Mediterranean. Much of the setting and symbolic bearings in Naimy's fictional and contemplative works, particularly *The Book of Mirdad*, derive from the majestic natural beauty and grandeur of the place. Naimy's varied education took him from his village Greek Orthodox school to the Teachers' Institute in Nazareth, Palestine; to the Theological Seminary in Poltava, Russia; and to the University of Washington, USA, where he received degrees in Liberal Arts and Law in 1916. After graduation, he moved to New York and, with Kahlil Gibran and eight other young literati, founded a dynamic movement which revolutionized Arabic literature. In 1932 and after the death of Kahlil Gibran, Naimy returned to his beloved Biskinta where he devoted himself entirely to writing until his death in 1988. His thirty-one books, acclaimed as classics throughout the Arab-speaking world, include drama, poetry, criticism, short stories, biography, autobiography and essays on the deeper meaning of human existence. Besides *The Book of Mirdad*, which has been widely translated, Naimy is known to the Western world for other works, mainly *Memoirs of a Vagrant Soul*, *Till We Meet* and his biography of Kahlil Gibran.

To,
Dr. Metin & Mrs. Buket
Aydemir
with love & respect.

Gautam Patel
8/30/03

# THE BOOK OF MIRDAD

A LIGHTHOUSE AND A HAVEN

---

## MIKHAIL NAIMY

## ARKANA

PENGUIN BOOKS

ARKANA

Published by the Penguin Group
Penguin Books Ltd, 27 Wrights Lane, London W8 5TZ, England
Penguin Books USA Inc., 375 Hudson Street, New York, New York 10014, USA
Penguin Books Australia Ltd, Ringwood, Victoria, Australia
Penguin Books Canada Ltd, 10 Alcorn Avenue, Toronto, Ontario, Canada M4V 3B2
Penguin Books (NZ) Ltd, 182–190 Wairau Road, Auckland 10, New Zealand

Penguin Books Ltd, Registered Offices: Harmondsworth, Middlesex, England

First published in Lebanon by Sader's Library 1948
First published in India by N. M. Tripathi Ltd 1954
First published in Great Britain by Stuart & Watkins Ltd 1962
Published by Penguin Books 1971
Reprinted by Arkana 1993
3  5  7  9  10  8  6  4

Printed in England by Clays Ltd, St Ives plc

# Contents

# Contents

# THE STORY OF THE BOOK

# The Bound Abbot

In the Milky Mountains, upon the lofty summit known as Altar Peak, stand the spacious and sombre ruins of a monastery once famous as THE ARK. Traditions would link it with an antiquity so hoary as the Flood.

Numerous legends have been woven about the Ark; but the one most current on the tongues of local mountaineers among whom I chanced to spend a certain summer in the shade of Altar Peak is the following:

Many years after the great Deluge Noah and his family, and his family's increase, drifted into the Milky Mountains where they found fertile valleys, abundant streams and a most equable climate. There they decided to settle.

When Noah felt his days drawing to an end he called unto him his son Sam who was a dreamer and a man of visions like himself, and spoke unto him saying:

'Behold, my son. Your father's harvest of years has been exceeding rich. Now is the last sheaf ready for the sickle. You and your brothers, and your children and your children's children shall repeople the bereaved Earth, and your seed shall be as the sand of the sea, according to God's promise unto me.

'Yet a certain fear besets my flickering days. It is that men shall in time forget the Flood and the lusts and wickednesses that brought it on. They shall also forget the Ark and the Faith that bore it in triumph for fifty and one hundred days over the furies of the revengeful deeps. Nor shall they be mindful of the New Life that issued of that Faith whereof they shall be the fruit.

'Lest they forget, I bid you, my son, to build an altar upon the highest peak in these mountains, which peak shall henceforth be known as Altar Peak. I bid you further build an house around that altar, which house shall correspond in all details to the ark, but in much reduced dimensions, and shall be known as The Ark.

'Upon that altar I propose to offer my last thanks offering. And from the fire I shall kindle thereon I bid you keep a light perpetually burning. As to the house, you shall make of it a sanctuary for a small

9

community of chosen men whose number shall never exceed nine, nor ever be less than nine. They shall be known as Ark Companions. When one of them dies, God will immediately provide another in his stead. They shall not leave the sanctuary, but shall be cloistered therein all their days, practising all the austerities of the Mother Ark, keeping the fire of faith burning and calling unto The Highest for guidance to themselves and to their fellow-men. Their bodily needs shall be provided them by the charity of the faithful.'

Sam, who had hung upon each syllable of his father's words, interrupted him to know the reason for the number *nine* – no more, no less. And the age-burdened patriarch explaining said:

'That is, my son, the number of those who sailed the Ark.'

But Sam could count no more than eight: His father and mother, himself and his wife, and his two brothers and their wives. Therefore was he much perplexed at his father's words. And Noah, perceiving his son's perplexity, explained further:

'Behold, I reveal unto you a great secret, my son. The ninth person was a stowaway, known and seen by me alone. He was my constant companion and my helmsman. Ask me no more of him, but fail not to make room for him in your sanctuary. These are my wishes, Sam, my son. See you to them.'

And Sam did according as his father commanded.

When Noah was gathered unto his fathers, his children buried him under the altar in the Ark which for ages thereafter continued to be, in deed and in spirit, the very sanctuary conceived and ordained by the venerable conqueror of the Flood.

In the course of centuries, however, the Ark began, by and by, to accept donations from the faithful far in excess of its needs. As a result it grew richer and richer every year in lands, in silver and gold, and in precious stones.

A few generations ago when one of the Nine had just passed away a stranger came to the gates and asked to be admitted into the community. According to the ancient traditions of the Ark which had never been violated the stranger should have been accepted at once, being the first to ask for admittance immediately following upon a companion's death. But the Senior, as the abbot of the Ark was called, chanced at the time to be a wilful, worldly-minded and hardhearted man. He did not like the stranger's appearance who was naked, famished and covered with wounds; and he told him that he was unworthy of admittance into the community.

The stranger insisted on being admitted, and this insistence on his part so infuriated the Senior that he bade him leave the grounds in haste. But the stranger was persuasive and would not be sent away. In the end he prevailed upon the Senior to take him in as a servant.

Long did the Senior wait thereafter upon Providence to send a companion in place of the one who died. But no man came. Thus, for the first time in its history, the Ark housed eight companions and a servant.

Seven years passed, and the monastery grew so rich that no one could assess its riches. It owned all the lands and villages for miles and miles about. The Senior was very happy, and became well disposed towards the stranger believing him to have brought 'good luck' to the Ark.

At the dawn of the eighth year, however, things began to change swiftly. The erstwhile peaceful community was in ferment. The clever Senior soon divined that the stranger was the cause, and decided to put him out. But alas, it was too late. The monks, under his leadership, were no longer amenable to any rule or reason. In two years they gave away all the properties of the monastery, personal and real. The monastery's innumerable tenants they made freeholders. At the third year they deserted the monastery. And what is more horrifying, the stranger laid a curse upon the Senior whereby he is *bound* to the grounds of the monastery and made dumb until this day.

Thus runs the legend.

There was no dearth of eyewitnesses who assured me that on many occasions – sometimes by day and sometimes by night – they had seen the Senior wandering about the grounds of the deserted and now much ruined monastery. Yet none was ever able to force a single word out of his lips. Moreover, each time he felt the presence of any man or woman he would quickly disappear no one knew where.

I confess that this story robbed me of my rest. The vision of a solitary monk – or even his shadow – wandering for many years in and about the courts of so ancient a sanctuary, upon a peak so desolate as Altar Peak, was too haunting to chase away. It teased my eyes; it smote my thoughts; it lashed my blood; it goaded my flesh and bone.

At last I said, I would ascend the mountain.

# Flint Slope

Facing the sea to the west and rising many thousands of feet above it, with a front broad, steep and craggy, Altar Peak appeared from a distance defying and forbidding. Yet two reasonably safe accesses were pointed out to me, both tortuous narrow paths and skirting many precipices – one from the south, another from the north. I decided to take neither. Between the two, descending directly from the summit and reaching almost to its very base, I could discern a narrow, smooth-faced slope which appeared to me as the road royal to the peak. It attracted me with an uncanny force, and I determined to make it my road.

When I revealed my determination to one of the local mountaineers he fixed me with two flaming eyes, and striking his hands together, shouted in terror,

'Flint Slope? Never be so foolish as to give your life away so cheap. Many have attempted it before you, but none ever returned to tell the tale. Flint Slope? – Never, never!'

With this he insisted on guiding me up the mountain. But I politely declined his help; I cannot explain why his terror had a reverse effect on me. Instead of deterring me it spurred me on and fixed me firmer than before in my purpose.

Of a certain morn, just as darkness was graying into light, I shook the night's dreams off my eyelids, and grasping my staff, with seven loaves of bread, I struck for Flint Slope. The low breath of the expiring night, the quick pulse of the day being born, a gnawing longing to face the mystery of the *bound* monk, and a still more gnawing one to unyoke myself from myself at least for a moment, no matter how brief, seemed to lend wings to my feet and buoyancy to my blood.

I began my journey with a song in my heart and a firm determination in my soul. But when, after a long and joyous march, I reached the lower end of the Slope and attempted to scale it with my eyes, I quietly swallowed my song. What appeared to me from a distance a straight, smooth, ribbon-like roadbed now stretched before me broad, and steep, and high, and unconquerable. So far as my eye could reach upward and sideward I could see nothing but broken flint of various sizes and shapes, the smallest chip a sharp needle or a whetted blade. Not a trace of life anywhere. A shroud so sombre as to be awe-inspiring hung over all the landscape about, while the summit was not to be glimpsed. Yet would I not be deterred.

With the eyes of the good man who warned me against the slope still flaming on my face, I called my determination forth and began my upward march. Soon, however, I realized that my feet alone could advance me no great distance; for the flint kept slipping from under them creating a horrific sound like a million throats labouring in a death throttle. To make any headway I had to dig my hands and knees, as well as my toes, in the mobile flint. How I wished then I had the agility of a goat!

Up and up I crawled in a zigzag, giving myself no rest. For I began to fear that night would overtake me before I reached my goal. To retreat was far from my mind.

The day was well nigh spent when I felt a sudden attack of hunger. Till then I had no thought of food or drink. The loaves of bread which I had tied in a handkerchief about my waist were too precious indeed to be valued at that moment. I untied them and was about to break the first morsel when the sound of a bell and what seemed like the wailing of a reed flute struck my ears. Nothing could be more startling in that flint-hoofed desolation.

Presently I saw a great black bellwether appear on a ridge to my right. Before I could catch my breath goats surrounded me on all sides, the flint crashing under their feet as under mine, but producing a much less horrifying sound. As though by invitation, the goats, led by the wether, dashed at my bread and would have snatched it from my hands had it not been for the voice of their shepherd who – I know not how and whence – appeared to be at my elbow. He was a youth of striking appearance – tall, strong and radiant. A loin skin was his only raiment, and the reed flute in his hand his only weapon:

'My bellwether is a spoiled goat', said he softly and smilingly. 'I feed him bread whenever I have it. But no bread-eating creatures have passed here in many, many moons.' Then turning to his leading goat, 'Do you see how good Fortune provides, my faithful bellwether? Never despair of Fortune.'

Whereupon he reached down and took a loaf. Believing that he was hungry I said to him very gently and very sincerely,

'We will share this frugal meal. There is enough bread for both of us – and for the bellwether.'

To my almost paralysing astonishment he threw the first loaf to the goats, then the second and third, and so until the seventh, taking a bite of each for himself. I was thunderstruck, and anger began to tear my chest. Yet realizing my helplessness, I quieted my anger in a measure, and turning a puzzled eye upon the goatherd said half-begging, half-reproaching,

'Now, that you have fed a hungry man's bread to your goats, would you not feed him some of their milk?'

'My goats' milk is poison to fools; and I would not have any of my goats guilty of taking even a fool's life.'

'But wherein am I a fool?'

'In that you take seven loaves of bread for a seven lives' journey.'

'Should I have taken seven thousand, then?'

'Not even one.'

'To go provisionless on such a long journey – is that what you advise?'

'The way that provides not for the wayfarer is no way to fare upon.'

'Would you have me eat flint for bread and drink my sweat for water?'

'Your flesh is food sufficient, and your blood is drink sufficient. There is the way besides.'

'You mock me, goatherd, overmuch. Yet would I not return your mockery. Whoever eats of my bread, although he leave me famished the same becomes my brother. The day is slipping down the mountain, and I must be on my way. Would you not tell me if I be still far from the summit?'

'You are too near Oblivion.'

With this he put the flute to his lips and marched off to the weird notes of a tune which sounded like a plaint from the nether worlds. The bellwether followed, and after him the rest of the goats. For a long space I could hear the crashing of the flint and the bleating of the goats mixed with the wailing of the flute.

Having entirely forgotten my hunger, I began to rebuild what the goatherd had destroyed of my energy and determination. If night were to find me in that dismal mass of flowing flint, I must seek me a place where I could stretch my tired bones without fear of rolling down the Slope. So I resumed my crawling. Looking down the mountain I could hardly believe that I had risen so high. The lower end of the Slope was no longer in sight. While the summit seemed almost within reach.

By nightfall I came to a group of rocks forming a kind of grotto. Although the grotto overhung an abyss whose bottom heaved with dreary, dark shadows, I decided to make it my lodging for the night.

My footgear was in shreds and heavily stained with blood. As I attempted to remove it I found that my skin had clung to it tightly, as if glued. The palms of my hands were covered with red furrows. The nails were like the edge of a bark torn off a dead tree. My clothes had donated their better parts to the sharp flints. My head was swelling with sleep. It seemed to contain no thought of anything else.

How long I had been asleep – a moment, an hour, or an eternity, I do not know. But I awakened feeling some force pulling at my sleeve. Sitting up, startled and sleep-dazed, I beheld a young maiden standing in front of me with a dimlighted lantern in hand. She was entirely naked and most delicately beauteous of face and form. Pulling at my jacket sleeve was an old woman as ugly as the maiden was beautiful. A cold shiver shook me from head to foot.

'Do you see how good Fortune provides, my sweet child?', the woman was saying as she half-pulled the jacket off my shoulders. 'Never despair of Fortune.'

I was tongue-tied and made no effort to speak, still less to resist. In vain I called upon my will. It seemed to have deserted me. So utterly powerless was I in the old woman's hands, although I could blow her and her child out of the grotto if I so wished. But I could not even wish, nor did I have the power to blow.

Not content with the jacket alone, the woman proceeded to undress me further until I was entirely naked. As she undressed me she would hand each garment to the maiden who would put it on herself. The shadow of my naked body thrown against the wall of the grotto, together with the two women's tattered shadows, filled me with fright and disgust. I watched without understanding, and stood speechless when speech was most urgent and the only weapon

left me in my unsavoury state. At last my tongue was loosened, and
I said:

'If you have lost all shame, old woman, I have not. I am ashamed
of my nakedness even before a shameless witch like you. But infinitely more ashamed am I before the maiden's innocence.'

'As she wears your shame, so wear her innocence.'

'What need has a maiden of a weary man's tattered clothes, and
one who is lost in the mountains at such a place, in such a night?'

'Perhaps to lighten his load. Perhaps to keep her warm. The poor
child's teeth are chattering with cold.'

'But when cold makes my teeth to click, wherewith shall I chase
it away? Have you no mercy in your heart? My clothes are all my
possessions in this world.'

'Less possessing – less possessed.

More possessing – more possessed.

More possessed – less assessed.

Less possessed – more assessed.

Let us be off, my child.'

As she took the maiden's hand and was about to go, a thousand
questions pressed upon my mind which I wished to ask her; but
only one came to the tip of my tongue:

'Before you leave, old woman, would you not be kind enough to
tell me if I be still far from the summit?'

'You are on the brink of the Black Pit.'

The lantern light flickered back to me their queer shadows as they
stepped out of the grotto and vanished in the sootblack night. A
dark chilly wave rushed at me I know not whence. Still darker and
more chilly waves followed. The very walls of the grotto seemed to
be breathing frost. My teeth chattered, and with them my already
muddled thoughts: The goats pasturing on flints, the mocking goatherd, this woman and this maiden; myself naked, bruised, cut,
famished, freezing, dazed, in such a grotto, on the edge of such an
abyss. Was I near my goal? Will I ever reach it? Will there be an
end to this night?

Hardly had I the time to collect myself when I heard the barking
of a dog and saw another light, so near, so near – right in the grotto.

'Do you see how good Fortune provides, my beloved? Never
despair of Fortune.' The voice was that of an old, very old man,

bearded, bent and shaky in the knees. He was addressing a woman old as himself, toothless, dishevelled and also bent and shaky in the knees. Taking apparently no note of my presence, he continued in the same squeaky voice that seemed to struggle out of his throat:

'A gorgeous nuptial chamber for our love, and a splendid staff in place of the one you lost. With such a staff you should not stumble any more, my love.' Saying that, he picked up my staff and handed it to the woman who bent over it in tenderness and stroked it caressingly with her withered hands. Then, as if taking note of me, but always speaking to his companion, he added:

'The stranger shall depart anon, beloved, and we shall dream our night's dreams all alone.'

This fell upon me as a command which I felt too impotent to disobey, especially when the dog approached me snarling menacingly as if to carry out his master's order. The whole scene filled me with terror, I watched it as in a trance; and as one entranced, I arose and walked to the entrance of the grotto, making the while desperate efforts to speak – to defend myself, to assert my right.

'My staff you have taken. Will you be so cruel as to take this grotto also which is my home for the night?'

'Happy are the staffless,
They stumble not.
Happy are the homeless,
They are at home.
The stumblers only – like ourselves,
Need walk with staffs.
The home-chained only, like ourselves,
Must have a home.'

So they chanted together as they prepared their couch, digging their long nails in the ground and levelling the gravel as they chanted, but paying no heed to me. This made me cry in desperation:

'Look at my hands. Look at my feet. I am a wayfarer, lost in this desolate slope. I traced my way hither in my own blood. Not an inch further can I see of this fearful mountain which seems to be so familiar to you. Have you no fear of retribution? Give me at least your lantern, if you will not permit me to share this grotto with you for the night.'

'Love will not be bared.
Light will not be shared.
Love and see.
Light and be.
When the night is bled,
And the day is fled.
And the earth is dead,
How shall wayfarers fare?
Who shall be there to dare?'

Utterly exasperated, I decided to resort to supplication, feeling all the while that it would be of no avail; for an uncanny force kept pushing me outside.

'Good old man. Good old woman. Though numb with cold and dumb with weariness, I shall not be a fly in your ointment. I, too, have tasted once of love. I shall leave you my staff and my humble lodging which you have chosen for your nuptial chamber. But one small thing do I ask of you in return: Since you deny me the light of you lantern, will you not be so gracious as to guide me out of this grotto and direct me towards the summit? For I have lost all sense of direction, and of balance as well. I know not how high I have risen, and how much higher I have yet to rise.'

Paying no heed to my supplications, they chanted on:
'The truly high is ever low.
The truly swift is ever slow.
The highly sensitive is numb.
The highly eloquent is dumb.
The ebb and flow are but one tide.
The guideless has the surest guide.
The very great is very small.
And he has all who gives his all."

As a last effort I besought them to tell me which way I should turn after leaving the grotto; for death might be lurking for me in the first step I should take; and I did not wish yet to die. Breathlessly I awaited their reply which came in another weird chant and left me more perplexed and exasperated than before:
'The brow of the rock is hard and steep.
The lap of the void is soft and deep.
The lion and the maggot,

19

The cedar and the fagot,
The rabbit and the snail,
The lizard and the quail,
The eagle and the mole –
All in one hole.
One hook. One bait.
Death alone can compensate.
As beneath, so on high –
Die to live, or live to die.'

The light of the lantern flickered off as I crawled out of the grotto on hands and knees, with the dog crawling behind me as though to make certain of my exit. Darkness was so heavy I could feel its black weight upon my eyelids. Not another moment could I tarry. The dog made me very certain of that.

One hesitant step. Another hesitant step. At the third I felt as if the mountain had suddenly slipped from under my feet, and I found me caught in the churning billows of a sea of darkness which sucked my breath and tossed me violently down – down, down.

The last vision that flashed through my mind as I whirled in the void of the Black Pit was that of the fiendish groom and bride. The last words I mumbled as the breath froze in my nostrils were their words,

'Die to live, or live to die.'

# The Keeper of The Book

'Arise, O happy stranger. You have attained your goal.'
Parched with thirst and squirming under the scorching rays of the sun, I half-opened my eyes to find me prostrate on the ground and to see the black figure of a man bending over me and gently moistening my lips with water, and as gently washing the blood off my many wounds. He was heavy of bulk, coarse of features, shaggy of beard and brow, deep and sharp of gaze, and of an age most difficult to determine. His touch withal was soft and strengthening. With his help I was able to sit up and to ask in a voice which barely reached my own ears,

'Where am I?'

'On Altar Peak.'

'And the grotto?'

'Behind you.'

'And the Black Pit?'

'In front of you.'

Great was my astonishment, indeed, when I looked and, in truth, found the grotto behind me and the black chasm yawning before me. I was on the very brink of it, and I asked the man to move with me into the grotto which he willingly did.

'Who brought me out of the Pit?'

'He who guided you up to the summit must have brought you out of the Pit.'

'Who is *he*?'

'The selfsame *he* who tied my tongue and kept me chained to this Peak for one hundred and fifty years.'

'Are you, then, the *bound* abbot?'

'I am he.'

'But you speak. He is dumb.'

'You have untied my tongue.'

'He also shuns the company of men. You do not seem at all afraid of me.'

'I shun all men but you.'

'You never saw my face before. How come you shun all men but me?'

'For one hundred and fifty years have I awaited your coming. For one hundred and fifty years omitting not a single day, in all seasons and in all weathers, my sinful eyes would search the flints of the Slope perchance I would see a man ascend this mountain and arrive here as you have arrived, staffless, naked and provisionless. Many have attempted the ascent by the Slope but none ever arrived. Many have arrived by other paths, but none staffless, naked and provisionless. I watched your progress all day yesterday. I let you sleep out the night at the grotto; but with the early dawn I came here and found you breathless. Yet was I certain that you would come to life. And, lo! You are more living than I. You have died to live. I am living to die. Aye, glory to *his* name. It is all as *he* promised. It is all as it should be. It leaves no question in my mind that you are the chosen man.'

'Who?'

'The blessed one into whose hands I should deliver the sacred book to publish to the world.'

'What Book?'

'*His* book – The Book of Mirdad.'

'Mirdad? Who is Mirdad?'

'Is it possible you have not heard of Mirdad? How strange. I was full certain that his name by now had filled the earth as it does fill until this day the ground beneath me, the air about me and the sky above me. Holy is this ground, O stranger, his feet trod it. Holy is this air; his lungs breathed it. Holy is this sky; his eyes scanned it.' Saying that, the monk bent reverently, kissed the ground three times, and fell silent. After a pause I said,

'You whet my appetite for more about this man you call Mirdad.'

'Lend me your ear, and I will tell you what is not forbidden me to tell. My name is Shamadam. I was Senior of the Ark when one of the nine companions died. Hardly had his soul departed hence when I was told that a stranger was at the gate asking for me. I knew at once that Providence had sent him to take the dead companion's place, and should have rejoiced that God was still watching over the Ark as He had done since the days of our father Sam.'

At this point I interrupted him to ask if what I was told by the people below were true, that the Ark was built by Noah's first son. His answer came quick and emphatic,

'Aye, it is even as you have been told.' Then continuing his interrupted story,

'Yea, I should have rejoiced. But for reasons entirely beyond my ken I found rebellion heaving in my chest. Even before I laid an eye on the stranger, my whole being fought against him. And I decided to reject him, fully realizing that in rejecting him I would be violating the inviolable traditions and rejecting Him Who sent him.

'When I opened the gate and saw him – a mere youth of no more than twenty-five – my heart bristled with daggers which I wished to thrust into him. Naked, apparently famished and devoid of all means of protection, even a staff, he looked most helpless. Yet a certain light upon his face made him appear more invulnerable than a knight in full armour and much more ancient than his years. My very bowels cried out against him. Every drop of blood in my veins wished to crush him. Ask me not for an explanation. Perhaps his penetrating eye did strip my soul naked, and it frightened me to see my soul unclothed before any man. Perhaps his purity unveiled my filth, and it grieved me to lose the veils which I had so long woven for my filth. For filth has ever loved her veils. Perhaps there was an ancient feud between his stars and mine. Who knows? Who knows? He alone can tell.

'I told him in a voice most blunt and pitiless that he could not be admitted into the community, and ordered him to leave the place forthwith. But he stood his ground and quietly counselled me to reconsider. His counsel I took as an insult and I spat upon his face. Again he stood his ground unflinchingly, and slowly wiping the spittle off his face, he once more counselled me to change my decision. As he wiped the spittle off his face I felt as if mine were being smeared with it. I also felt myself defeated, and somewhere in the depth of me admitted that the combat was unequal, and that he was the stronger combatant.

'Like all defeated pride, mine would not give up the fight until it saw itself sprawled out and trampled in the dust. I was almost ready to grant the man's request. But I wished to see him humbled first. Yet would he not be humbled in any way.

'Suddenly he asked for some food and clothing, and my hopes revived. With hunger and cold arrayed against him on my side, I believed my battle won. Cruelly I refused to give him a morsel of bread saying that the monastery lived by charity and could dispense no charity. In that I lied most flagrantly; for the monastery was far too rich to deny food and clothing to the needy. I wanted him to beg. But he would not beg. He demanded as of right; there was commanding in his asking.

'The battle lasted long, but never swayed. From the beginning it was his. To cover my defeat I finally proposed to him to enter the Ark as a servant – as a servant only. That, I consoled myself, would humble him. Even then I did not realize that I was the beggar and not he. To seal my humiliation he accepted the proposal without a murmur. Little did I imagine at the time that by taking him in – even as a servant – I was putting myself out. Until the last day I clung to my delusion that I, and not he, was the master of the Ark. Ah, Mirdad, Mirdad, what have you done to Shamadam! Shamadam, what have you done to yourself!'

Two large tears trickled down the man's beard, and his great frame shook. My heart was moved, and I said,

'Speak no more, I pray you, of this man whose memory flows out of you in tears.'

'Be not disturbed, O blessed messenger. It is the Senior's pride of yore that is distilling yet these tears of gall. It is the authority of the letter that is gnashing its teeth against the authority of the spirit. Let the pride weep; it weeps its last. Let the authority gnash; it gnashes for the last time. Ah, that my eyes were not so veiled in earthly mist when they first beheld his celestial countenance! Ah, that my ears were not so clogged with the wisdom of the world when they were challenged by his divine wisdom! Ah, that my tongue were not so coated with the bitter sweets of the flesh when it battled his spirit-coated tongue! But I have reaped much, and am yet to reap more, of the tares of my delusion.

'For seven years he was a lowly servant in our midst – gentle, alert, inoffensive, unobtrusive, ready to do any companion's slightest bidding. He moved about as if on air. Not a word escaped his lips. We believed him to have taken a vow of silence. Some of us were inclined at first to tease him. He met their thrusts with an unearthly calm, and soon forced us all to respect his silence. Unlike the other seven Companions who delighted in his calm and were soothed thereby, I found it oppressive and unnerving. Many an effort did I make to disturb it, but all in vain.

'His name he gave us as Mirdad. To that name only he responded. That was all we knew of him. Yet was his presence keenly felt by all, so keenly that seldom we would speak, even of things essential, save after he retired into his cell.

'They were years of plenty, the first seven years of Mirdad. Sevenfold and more were the monastery's vast possessions increased. My heart softened towards him, and I seriously consulted the community upon admitting him as a companion, seeing that Providence sent us no one else.

'Just then occurred what no one did foresee – what no one could foresee, and least of all this poor Shamadam. Mirdad unsealed his lips, and the tempest was unleashed. He gave vent to what his silence had so long concealed, and it burst forth in torrents so irresistible that all Companions were caught in their sweeping rush – all save this poor Shamadam who fought them to the last. I sought to turn the tide by asserting my authority as Senior, but the Companions would recognize no authority save that of Mirdad. Mirdad was the master; Shamadam, but an outcast. I resorted even to cunning. To some companions I offered rich bribes of silver and of gold; to others I promised large tracts of fertile land. I had almost succeeded when, in some mysterious manner, Mirdad became aware of my labours and undid them without an effort – simply with a few words.

'Too strange and too involved was the doctrine he held forth. It is all in The Book. Of that I am not allowed to speak. But his eloquence would make the snow appear as pitch, and the pitch as snow. So keen and forceful was his word. To that weapon what could I oppose? Nothing at all except the monastery's seal which was in my keeping. But even that was rendered of no use. For the Companions, under his flaming exhortations, would force me to set my hand and the monastery's seal to every document they saw fit to have me execute. Bit by bit they deeded away the lands of the monastery which had been donated by the faithful over a stretch of ages. Then began Mirdad to send the Companions out, laden with gifts to the poor and needy in all the villages hereabout. On the last Day of the Ark, which was one of the two annual festivals of the Ark – the other being The Day of The Vine – Mirdad concluded his mad acts by ordering his Companions to strip the monastery clean of all effects and to distribute them to the people gathered without.

'All that I witnessed with my sinful eyes, and recorded in my heart that was about to burst with hatred for Mirdad. If hate alone could slay, that which was then seething in my breast should have slain a thousand Mirdads. But his love was stronger than my hate. Again the combat was unequal. Again my pride would not desist until it saw itself sprawled out and trampled in the dust. He crushed me without fighting me. I fought him, but only crushed myself. How often he would try in his long, loving patience to remove the scales which were upon my eyes! How often I would look for more and tougher scales to paste upon my eyes! The more of his gentleness he offered me, the more I gave him of my hatred in return.

'We were two warriors in the field – Mirdad and I. He was a legion in himself. I fought a lonely fight. Had I the help of the other Companions, I should have conquered in the end. And then I would have eaten out his heart. But my companions fought with him against me. The traitors! Mirdad, Mirdad, you have avenged yourself.'

More tears, accompanied this time by sobs, and a long pause after which the Senior once more bent and three times kissed the ground, saying,

'Mirdad, my conqueror, my lord, my hope, my punishment and my reward, forgive Shamadam's bitterness. A snake's head keeps its poison even after it's severed from the body. But happily it cannot bite. Behold, Shamadam is now fangless and poisonless. Sustain him with your love that he may see the day when his mouth shall drip with honey like your mouth. For that he has your promise. You have this day delivered him of his first prison. Let him not tarry long in the second.'

As if he read the question in my mind as to the prisons he had spoken of, the Senior sighingly explained, but in a voice so mellowed and so changed that one could truly swear it was another man's,

'Upon that day he called us all into this very grotto where often was his wont to teach the Seven. The sun was about to set. The west wind had driven up a heavy mist that filled the gorges and hung like a mystic shroud over all the land from here to the sea. It reached no higher than the waist of our mountain which had the appearance of having become a seashore. On the western horizon spread grim and heavy clouds that entirely obscured the sun. The Master, moved, but bridling his emotions, embraced each of the Seven in turn, saying as he embraced the last:

'Long have you lived upon the heights. To-day must you descend into the depths. Save you ascend by descending, and save you join the valley to the summit, the heights shall ever make you giddy, and the depths shall ever make you blind.'

'Turning then to me, he looked long and tenderly into my eyes and said:

' "As to you, Shamadam, your hour is not yet. You shall await my coming on this peak. And while awaiting me you shall be the keeper of my book, which is locked within an iron chest beneath the altar. See that no hands touch it – not even yours. In due time I shall send my messenger to take it and to publish it unto the world. By these signs shall you know him: He shall ascend this summit by the slope of flints. He shall have started on his journey hither fully clothed, provided with a staff and seven loaves of bread; but you shall find him in front of this grotto staffless, provisionless and naked, and also devoid of breath. Until his coming your tongue and lips shall be sealed, and you shall shun all human company. The sight of him alone shall release you from the prison of silence. After delivering the Book into his hands you shall be turned into a stone, which stone shall guard the entrance to this grotto until my coming. From that prison I alone shall deliver you. Should you find the waiting long, it shall be made longer. Should you find it short, it shall be made shorter. Believe and be patient.' Whereupon he embraced me also.

'Then turning again to the Seven, he waved his hand and said, "Companions, follow me."

'And he marched before them down the Slope, his noble head uplifted, his steady gaze searching the distance, his holy feet barely hitting the ground. When they had reached the rim of the pall of mist the sun broke through the lower edge of the black cloud over the sea, forming a vaulted passage in the sky illumined with a light too wondrous for human words, too blinding for mortal eyes. And it looked to me as if the Master with the Seven had been detached from the mountain and were walking on the mist straight into the vault – into the sun. And it grieved me to be left behind alone – ah, so alone.'

Like one exhausted by the heavy labours of a long day, Shamadam suddenly relaxed and fell silent, his head drooping, his eyelids shut, his chest heaving in uneven turns. So he remained for a long space. As I searched my mind for some consoling words, he raised his head and said:

'You are beloved of Fortune. Forgive an unfortunate man. I have spoken much – perhaps too much. How could I otherwise? Can one whose tongue has fasted for one hundred and fifty years break his fast with but an "yea" or "nay"? Can a Shamadam be a Mirdad?'

'Allow me a question, brother Shamadam.'

'How good of you to call me "brother". No one has called me by that name since my only brother died, and that was many years ago. What is your question?'

'Since Mirdad is so great a teacher, I am astonished that until this day the world has not heard of him or any of his seven companions. How can that be?'

'Perhaps, he is biding his time. Perhaps he teaches under some other name. Of one thing am I certain: Mirdad will change the world as he has changed the Ark.'

'He must have died a long time since.'

'Not Mirdad. Mirdad is mightier than death.'

'Do you imply he will destroy the world as he destroyed the Ark?'

'Nay, and nay again! He will unburden the world as he unburdened our Ark. And then will he relight the everlasting light which men like me have hid under too many bushels of delusions, and now bemoan the darkness they are in. He will rebuild in men what men have demolished of themselves. The Book shall soon be in your hands. Read it and see the light. I must delay no longer. Wait here a while till I return, you must not come with me.'

He arose and hastily went out, leaving me quite bewildered and impatient. I, too, stepped out, but went no further than the edge of the abyss.

The magic lines and colours of the scene spread out before my eyes so gripped my soul that for a moment I felt myself dissolved and sprayed in drops imperceptible over and into everything: Over the sea in the distance, calm and empalled by pearly haze; over the hills, now bending, now reclining, but all rising in rapid succession from the shore and steadily pushing upwards to the very crests of the rugged peaks; over the peaceful settlements upon the hills framed in the greenness of the earth; over the verdant valleys nestling in the hills, quenching their thirst from the liquid hearts of the mountains and studded with men at labour and beasts at pasture; into the gorges and ravines, the mountains' living scars in their battle with Time; into the languid breeze; into the azure sky above; into the ashen earth below.

Only when my eyes in their roaming had come to rest upon the Slope was I brought back to the monk and his abashing narrative of himself and of Mirdad and the Book. And I marvelled greatly at the hand unseen that set me out in search of one thing only to lead me to another. And I blessed it in my heart.

Presently the monk returned and, handing me a small parcel wrapped in a piece of age-yellowed linen cloth, said,

'My trust is henceforth your trust. Be faithful in your trust. Now is my second hour at hand. The gates of my prison are swinging open to receive me. Soon will they swing shut to enclose me. How long will they remain shut – Mirdad only can tell. Soon will Shamadam be effaced from every memory. How painful, ah, how painful it is to be effaced! Why say I that? Nothing is ever effaced from Mirdad's memory. Whoever lives in Mirdad's memory, the same forever lives.'

A long pause followed after which the Senior lifted his head and looking at me with his tear-dimmed eyes resumed in a barely audible whisper,

'Presently you shall descend into the world. But you are nude, and the world abhors nudity. Its very soul it wraps in rags. My clothes are no longer of use to me. I go into the grotto to shed them that you may cover your nudity therewith, albeit Shamadam's clothes can fit no man except Shamadam. May they not prove entanglements to you.'

I made no comment on the proposal, accepting it in glad silence. As the Senior went into the grotto to disrobe I unwrapped the Book and fumblingly began to turn its yellow parchment leaves. Quickly I found myself arrested by the first page I made an effort to read. I read on and on, becoming more and more absorbed. Subconsciously

I was waiting upon the Senior to anounce that he had finished un-
dressing and to call me to dress. But minutes passed, and he did not
call.

Lifting my eyes from the pages of the Book I looked into the
grotto and saw in the middle of it the heap of the Senior's clothes.
But the Senior himself was not to be seen. I called him several times,
each time louder than before. There was no response. I was much
alarmed and most bewildered. There was no exit from the grotto
save through the narrow entrance where I was standing. The Senior
did not go out through the entrance – of that I was certain beyond
the slightest doubt. Was he an apparition? But I felt his flesh and
bone with my own bone and flesh. Besides, there was the Book in
my hands, and the clothes inside the grotto. Is he perchance beneath
them? I went and picked them up, piece by piece, and ridiculed
myself as I picked them. Many more heaps like them would not
cover the bulky Senior. Did he, in some mysterious manner, slip
out of the grotto and fall into the Black Pit?

So quickly as the last thought flashed through my mind I dashed
outside; as quickly was I pinned to the ground a few steps outside
the entrance when I found me facing a great boulder right on the
edge of the Pit. The boulder was not there before. It had the
appearance of a crouching beast, but with a head bearing a striking
human likeness, of coarse and heavy features, the chin broad and
uplifted, the jaws firmly locked, the lips tightly shut, the eyes
squintingly peering into the vacant north.

# THE BOOK

This is the Book of
MIRDAD
as recorded by
*Naronda*
the youngest
and the least
of his companions,
a lighthouse
and a haven
for those who yearn
to overcome.
*Let all others
Beware of it!*

# CHAPTER ONE

## Mirdad Unveils Himself
## and Speaks on Veils and Seals

*Naronda*: Upon that eve the Eight were gathered round the supper board with Mirdad standing to one side and silently awaiting orders.

One of the ancient rules for Companions was to avoid, so much as possible, the use of the word *I* in their speech. Companion Shamadam was boasting of his achievements as Senior. He cited many figures showing how much he had added to the wealth and prestige of the Ark. In doing that he made excessive use of the forbidden word. Companion Micayon gently reprimanded him. Whereupon a heated discussion arose as to the purpose of the rule and who had laid it down, whether father Noah or the First Companion, meaning Sam. The heat led to recriminations, and recriminations to a general confusion where much was said and nothing understood.

Wishing to change confusion into mirth, Shamadam turned to Mirdad and said in evident derision:

'Behold, a greater than the patriarch is here. Mirdad, show us the way out of this maze of words.'

All eyes were turned upon Mirdad. And great were our astonishment and joy when, for the first time in seven years, he opened his mouth and spoke unto us saying,

MIRDAD: Companions of the Ark! Shamadam's wish, though uttered in derision, unwittingly foretells Mirdad's solemn decision. For since the day he came into this Ark Mirdad forechose this very time and place – this very circumstance – in which to break his seals, and cast away his veils, and stand revealed before you and the world.

With seven seals has Mirdad sealed his lips. With seven veils has Mirdad veiled his face, that he may teach you and the world, when you are ripe for teaching, how to unseal your lips and to unveil your eyes, and thus reveal yourselves to yourselves in fulness of the glory which is yours.

Your eyes are veiled with far too many veils. Each thing you look upon is but a veil.

Your lips are sealed with far too many seals. Each word you utter forth is but a seal.

For things, whatever be their form and kind, are only veils and swaddling-bands wherewith is Life enswaddled and enveiled. How can your eye, which is itself a veil and a swaddling-band, lead you to aught but swaddling-bands and veils?

And words – are they not things sealed up in letters and in syllables? How can your lip, which is itself a seal, give utterance to aught but seals?

The eye can veil, but cannot pierce the veils.

The lip can seal, but cannot break the seals.

Demand no more of either one of them. That is their portion of the body's labours; and they perform it well. By drawing veils, and by setting seals they call aloud to you to come and seek what is behind the veils, and to pry out what is beneath the seals.

To pierce the veils you need an eye other than that shaded with lash, and lid, and brow.

To break the seals you need a lip other than the familiar piece of flesh below your nose.

First *see* the eye itself aright, if you would see the other things aright. Not with the eye, but through it must you look that you may see all things beyond it.

Speak first the lip and tongue aright if you would speak the other words aright. Not with the lip and tongue, but through them must you speak that you may speak all words beyond them.

Did you but see and speak aright, you should see nothing but yourselves and utter nothing but yourselves. For in all things and beyond all things, as in all words and beyond all words, are you – the seer and the speaker.

If, then, your world be such a baffling riddle, it is because you are that baffling riddle. And if your speech be such a woeful maze, it is because you are that woeful maze.

Let things alone and labour not to change them. For they seem what they seem only because you seem what you seem. They neither see nor speak except you lend them sight and speech. If they be harsh of speech, look only to your tongue. If they be ugly of appearance, search first and last your eye.

Ask not of things to shed their veils. Unveil yourselves, and things will be unveiled. Nor ask of things to break their seals. Unseal your selves, and all will be unsealed.

The key to self-unveiling and self-unsealing is a word which you forever hold between your lips. Of words it is the slightest and the greatest. Mirdad has called it THE CREATIVE WORD.

*Naronda*: The Master paused; and silence deep, but vibrant with suspense, fell upon all. At last Micayon spoke in passionate impatience.

*Micayon*: Our ears are hungry for THE WORD. Our hearts are yearning for the key. Say on, we pray, Mirdad, say on.

# CHAPTER TWO

# On the Creative Word.
## *I* is the Source and Centre
## of All Things

MIRDAD: When you say *I*, say forthwith in your heart, 'God be my refuge from the woes of *I* and be my guide unto the bliss of *I*.' For in that word, albeit so very slight, is locked the soul of every other word. Unlock it once, and fragrant is your mouth, and sweet the tongue therein; each word of it shall drip with Life's delights. Let it remain locked up, and foul is the mouth, and bitter is the tongue; from every word of it shall ooze the pus of Death.

For *I*, O monks, is the Creative Word. And save you grasp thereof the magic power; and save you be of that power the masters, you are too apt to groan when you would sing; or be at war, when you would be at peace; or cringe in gaols dark, when you would soar in light.

Your *I* is but your consciousness of being, silent and incorporeal, made vocal and corporeal. It is the inaudible in you made audible, and the invisible made visible; that, seeing, you may see the unseeable; and hearing, you may hear the unhearable. For eye- and ear-bound yet are you. And save you see with eyes, and save you hear with ears, you see and hear nothing at all.

By merely thinking *I* you cause a sea of thoughts to heave within your heads. That sea is the creation of your *I* which is at once the thinker and the thought. If you have thoughts that sting, or stab, or claw, know that the *I* in you alone endowed them with sting and tusk and claw.

Mirdad would have you know as well that that which can endow can also disendow.

By merely feeling *I* you tap a well of feelings in your hearts. That well is the creation of your *I* which is at once the feeler and the felt. If there be briars in your hearts, know that the *I* in you alone has rooted them therein.

Mirdad would have you know as well that that which can so readily root in, the same can as readily root out.

By merely saying *I* you bring to life a mighty host of words; each word a symbol of a thing; each thing a symbol of a world; each world a part component of an universe. That universe is the creation of your *I* which is at once the maker and the made. If there be some hobgoblins in your universe, know that the *I* in you alone has brought them into being.

Mirdad would have you know as well that that which can create can also uncreate.

As the creator, so is the creation. Can anyone overcreate himself? Or anyone undercreate himself? Himself alone – no more, no less – does the creator procreate.

A fountainhead is *I* whence flow all things and whither they return. As is the fountainhead, so also is the flow.

A magic wand is *I*. Yet can the wand give birth to naught save what's in the magician. As is the magician, so are the products of his wand.

As is your Consciousness, therefore, so is your *I*. As is your *I*, so is your world. If it be clear and definite of meaning, your world is clear and definite of meaning; and then your words should never be a maze; nor should your deeds be ever nests of pain. If it be hazy and uncertain, your world is hazy and uncertain; and then your words are but entanglements; and then your deeds are hatcheries of pain.

If it be constant and enduring, your world is constant and enduring; then are you mightier than Time, and much more spacious than the Space. If it be passing and inconstant, your world is passing and inconstant; and then are you a wisp of smoke breathed upon lightly by the sun.

If it be one, your world is one; and then are you at everlasting peace with all the hosts of heaven and the tenants of the Earth. If it be many, your world is many; and then are you at an unending war with your very self and every creature in God's imcompassable domain.

*I* is the centre of your life whence radiate the things that make the total of your world, and whereunto they converge. If it be steady, your world is steady: then no powers above, and no powers below can sway you right or left. If it be shifting, your world is shifting; and then are you a helpless leaf caught in an angry whirl of wind.

And, lo! Your world is steady, to be sure; but only in unsteadiness.

And certain is your world, but only in uncertainty. And constant is your world, but only in inconstancy. And single is your world, but only in unsingleness.

Yours is a world of cradles turning into tombs, and tombs becoming cradles; of days devouring nights, and nights regurgitating days; of peace declaring war, and war suing for peace; of smiles afloat on tears, and tears aglow with smiles.

Yours is a world in constant travail, with Death as the midwife.

Yours is a world of sieves and cribbles, with no two sieves and cribbles alike. And you are ever at pains sifting the unsiftable and cribbling the uncribblable.

Yours is a world divided 'gainst itself, because the *I* in you is so divided.

Yours is a world of barriers and fences, because the *I* in you is one of barriers and fences. Some things it would fence out as alien to itself. Some things it would fence in as kindred to itself. Yet that outside the fence is ever breaking in; and that within the fence is ever breaking out. For they, being offspring of the same mother – even your *I* – would not be set apart.

And you, rather than joy in their happy union, begird yourselves anew for the fruitless labour of separating the inseparable. Rather than bind the cleavage in the *I*, you whittle away your life hoping to make thereof a wedge to drive between what you believe to be your *I* and what you imagine other than your *I*.

Therefore are men's words dipped in poison. Therefore are their days so drunken with sorrow. Therefore are their nights so tortured with pain.

Mirdad, O monks, would bind the cleavage in your *I* that you may live at peace with yourselves – with all men – with the universe entire.

Mirdad would draw the poison from your *I* that you may taste the sweetness of Understanding.

Mirdad would teach you how to weigh your *I* so as to know the joy of PERFECT BALANCE.

*Naronda*: Again the Master paused, and again deep silence fell on all. Once more Micayon broke the silence, saying,

*Micayon*: Too tantalizing are your words, Mirdad. They open many doors, but leave us on the threshold. Lead us beyond – lead us within.

40

# CHAPTER THREE

## The Holy Triune
## And the Perfect Balance

MIRDAD: Though each of you be centred in his *I*, yet are you all encentred in one *I* – even the single *I* of God.

God's *I*, O monks, is God's eternal, only word. In it is God – The Consciousness Supreme – made manifest. Without it He would be a silence absolute. By it is the Creator self-created. By it is the Formless One made to take on a multiplicity of forms through which the creatures shall pass again to formlessness.

To feel Himself; to think Himself; to speak Himself God need not utter more than *I*. Therefore is *I* His only word. Therefore is it THE WORD.

When God says *I*, nothing is left unsaid. Worlds seen and worlds unseen; things born, and things awaiting birth; time rolling by and time as yet to roll – all, all, excepting not a grain of sand, are uttered forth and pressed into that Word. By it were all things made. Through it are all sustained.

Except it have a meaning, a word is but an echo in the void.

Except its meaning be forever one, it is but cancer in the throat and pimples on the tongue.

God's Word is not an echo in the void, nor a cancer in the throat, nor pimples on the tongue except for those devoid of Understanding. For Understanding is the Spirit Holy that vivifies the Word and binds it unto Consciousness. It is the rider-beam of the balance Eternal whose two pans are The Primal Consciousness and The Word.

The Primal Consciousness – The Word – The Spirit of Understanding – behold, O monks, The TRINITY OF BEING, The Three which are One, The One which is Three, co-equal, co-extensive, co-eternal; self-balancing, self-knowing, self-fulfilling, Never increasing, nor decreasing. Ever at peace. Ever the same. That is, O monks, THE PERFECT BALANCE.

Man names it God, although it is too wondrous to be named. Yet holy is this name, and holy is the tongue that keeps it holy.

Now, what is Man if not an offspring of this God? Can he be different from God? Is not the oak enswathed within the acorn? Is not God wrapt in Man?

Man, too, therefore, is such an holy triune; a consciousness, a word, an understanding. Man, too, is a creator like his God. His *I* is his creation. Why is he not so balanced as his God?

If you would know the answer to this riddle, hear well what Mirdad shall reveal.

# CHAPTER FOUR

# Man is a God in Swaddling-bands

MAN is a god in swaddling-bands. Time is a swaddling-band. Space is a swaddling-band. Flesh is a swaddling-band, and likewise all the senses and the things perceivable therewith. The mother knows too well that the swaddling-bands are not the babe. The babe, however, knows it not.

Man is too conscious yet of his swaddles which change from day to day and from age to age. Hence is his consciousness ever in flux; and hence his word which is his consciousness expressed is never clear and definite of meaning; and hence his understanding is in fog; and hence is his life out of balance. It is confusion thrice confounded.

And so Man pleads for help. His agonizing cries reverberate throughout the aeons. The air is heavy with his moans. The sea is salty with his tears. The earth is furrowed with his tombs. The heavens are deafened with his prayers. And all because he knows not yet the meaning of his *I* which is to him the swaddling-bands as well as the babe therein enswaddled.

In saying *I* Man cleaves the Word in twain: his swaddling-bands, the one; God's deathless self, the other. Does Man in truth divide the Indivisible? God forbid. The Indivisible no power can divide – not even God's. Man's immaturity imagines the division. And Man, the infant, girds himself for battle and wages war upon the infinite All-Self believing it to be the enemy of his being.

In this unequal fight Man tears his flesh in shreds, and spills his blood in streams. While God, the Father-Mother, lovingly looks on. For He knows well that Man is tearing but the heavy veils, and spilling but the bitter gall that blind him to his oneness with the One.

That is Man's destiny – to fight and bleed and faint, and in the end to wake and bind the cleavage in the *I* with his own flesh and and seal it with his blood.

Therefore, O monks, have you been cautioned – and very wisely cautioned – to be chary in the use of *I*. For so long as you mean thereby the swaddling-bands and not the babe alone; so long as it is for you a cribble rather than a crucible, just so long will you be cribbling vanity, only to gather Death with all his brood of agonies and pains.

# CHAPTER FIVE

## On Crucibles and Cribbles
## God's Word and Man's

A CRUCIBLE is the Word of God. What it creates it melts and fuses into one, accepting none as worthy, rejecting none as worthless. Having the Spirit of Understanding, it knows full well that its creation and itself are one; that to reject a part is to reject the whole; and to reject the whole is to reject itself. Therefore is it forever one of purpose and purport.

Whereas a cribble is Man's word. What it creates it sets at grips and blows. It is forever picking this as friend and casting that away as enemy. And but too oft its friend of yesterday becomes the enemy of to-day; the enemy of to-day, the friend of to-morrow.

Thus rages on the cruel and the fruitless war of Man against himself. And all because Man lacks the Holy Spirit, the which alone can make him understand that he and his creation are but one; that to cast out the foe is to cast out the friend. For both words 'foe' and 'friend' are the creation of his word – his *I*.

What you dislike and cast away as evil is surely liked and picked up by someone, or something else as good. Can one thing be at once two self-excluding things? Neither is it the one, nor the other, excepting that your *I* has made it evil; another *I* has made it good.

Did I not say that that which can create can also uncreate? As you create an enemy so can you uncreate him, or re-create him as a friend. For that your *I* must needs be a crucible. For that you need the Spirit of Understanding.

Therefore I say to you that if you pray for anything at all, pray first and last for Understanding.

Never be cribblers, my companions. For the Word of God is Life, and Life is a crucible wherein all is made an oneness indivisible; all is at perfect equilibrium, and all is worthy of its author – The Holy Trinity. How much more worthy must it be of you?

Never be cribblers, my companions, and you shall stand in statures so immense, so all-pervading and so all-embracing, that no cribbles can be found to contain you.

Never be cribblers, my companions. Seek first the knowledge of The Word that you may know your own word. And when you know your word, you shall consign your cribbles to the fire. For your word and God's are one except that yours is still in veils.

Mirdad would have you cast away the veils.

God's Word is Time untimed, and Space unspaced. Was there a time when you were not with God? Is there a place where you are not in God? Why chain you, then, eternity with hours and with seasons? And why corral the Space in inches and in miles?

God's Word is Life unborn, therefore, undying. Wherefore is yours beset with birth and death? Are you not living by God's life alone? And can the Deathless be the source of Death?

God's word is all-inclusive. Nor barriers nor fences are therein. Wherefore is yours so rent with fence and barrier?

I say to you, your very flesh and bone are not the bone and flesh of you alone. Innumerable are the hands that dip with you in the same fleshpots of earth and sky whence come your bone and flesh and whither they return.

Nor is the light in your eyes the light of you alone. It is as well the light of all that share the Sun with you. What could your eye behold of me were it not for the light in me? It is *my* light that sees me in your eye. It is *your* light that sees you in my eye. Were I a total darkness your eye, looking at me, would be a total darkness.

Nor is the breath within your breast the breath of you alone. All those that breathe, or ever breathed the air are breathing in your breast. Is it not Adam's breath that still inflates your lungs? Is it not Adam's heart that is still beating in your hearts?

Nor are your thoughts the thoughts of you alone. The sea of common thought does claim them as her own; and so do all the thinking beings who share that sea with you.

Nor are your dreams the dreams of you alone. The universe entire is dreaming in your dreams.

Nor is your house the house of you alone. It is as well the dwelling of your guest, and of the fly, the mouse, the cat and all the creatures that share the house with you.

Beware, therefore, of fences. You but fence in Deception and fence out the Truth. And when you turn about to see yourselves

46

within the fence, you find you face to face with Death which is Deception by another name.

Inseparable, O monks, is Man from God; therefore, inseparable from his fellow-men and all the creatures that issue from The Word.

The Word is the ocean; you, the clouds. And is a cloud a cloud save for the ocean it contains? Yet foolish, indeed, is the cloud that would waste away its life striving to pin itself in space so as to keep its shape and its identity for ever. What would it reap of its so foolish striving but disappointed hopes and bitter vanity? Except it lose itself, it cannot find itself. Except it die and vanish as a cloud, it cannot find the ocean in itself which is its only self.

A God-bearing cloud is Man. Save he be emptied of himself, he cannot find himself. Ah, the joy of being empty!

Save you be lost forever in The Word you cannot understand the word which is you – even your *I*. Ah, the joy of being lost!

Again I say to you, Pray for Understanding. When Holy Understanding finds your hearts, there shall be naught in God's immensity that shall not ring to you a glad response each time you utter *I*.

And then shall Death himself be but a weapon in your hands wherewith to vanquish Death. And then shall Life bestow upon your hearts the key into her boundless heart. That is the golden key of Love.

*Shamadam*: I never dreamed that so much wisdom could be wrung out of a dishrag and a broom. (Alluding to Mirdad's position as a servant.)

MIRDAD: All is a store of wisdom for the wise. To the unwise wisdom herself is folly.

*Shamadam*: You have a clever tongue, no doubt. A wonder you have bridled it so long. Your words, albeit, are much too hard to hear.

MIRDAD: My words are easy, Shamadam. It is your ear that's hard. But woe to them who, hearing, do not hear; and woe to them who, seeing, do not see.

*Shamadam*: I hear and see too well; perhaps, too much. Yet would I not hear such a folly that Shamadam is the same as Mirdad; that the master and the servant are alike.

# CHAPTER SIX

## On Master and Servant
## Companions give Opinions of Mirdad

MIRDAD: Mirdad is not Shamadam's only servant. Can you, Shamadam, count your servants?

Is there an eagle or a falcon; is there a cedar or an oak; is there a mountain or a star; is there an ocean or a lake; is there an angel or a king that do not serve Shamadam? Is not the whole world in Shamadam's service?

Nor is Mirdad Shamadam's only master. Can you, Shamadam, count your masters?

Is there a beetle or a flea; is there an owl or a sparrow; is there a thistle or twig; is there a pebble or shell; is there a dewdrop or a pond; is there a beggar or a thief that are not served by Shamadam? Is not Shamadam in the whole world's service? For in doing its work the world does yours also. And in doing your work you do the world's work too.

Aye, the head is master of the belly. But no less is the belly master of the head.

Nothing can serve save it be served by serving. And nothing can be served except it serve the serving.

I say to you, Shamadam, and to all, The servant is the master's master. The master is the servant's servant. Let not the servant bow his head. Let not the master raise it high. Crush out the deadly master's pride. Root out the shameful servant's shame.

Remember that the Word is one. And you, as syllables in The Word, are in reality but one. No syllable is nobler than the other, nor more essential than the other. The many syllables are but a single syllable – even The Word. Such monosyllables must you become if you would know the passing ecstasy of that unutterable Self-Love which is a love for all – for everything.

Not as a master to his servant, nor as a servant to his master do I now speak to you, Shamadam; but as a brother to a brother. Wherefore are you so troubled by my words?

Deny me if you will. I will deny you not. Did I not say a while since that the flesh upon my back was no other than that upon your back? I would not stab you lest I bleed. So sheathe your tongue, if you would spare your blood. Unlock your heart to me if you would have it locked against all pain.

Better by far to be without a tongue than to have one whose words are snares and briars. And words shall always wound and snare until the tongue be cleansed by Holy Understanding.

I bid you search your hearts, O monks. I bid you tear all barriers therein. I bid you cast away the swaddling-bands wherewith your *I* is still enswaddled that you may see it as one with The Word of God, eternally at peace with itself and all the worlds that issue out of it.

So taught I Noah.

So I teach you.

*Naronda*: Thereupon Mirdad withdrew into his cell leaving us all exceedingly abashed. After a space of almost crushing silence companions started to disperse, each giving as he left his estimate of Mirdad.

*Shamadam*: A beggar dreaming of a kingly crown.

*Micayon*: He is the Stowaway. Did he not say, 'So taught I Noah'?

*Abimar*: A spool of tangled thread.

*Micaster*: A star of another firmament.

*Bennoon*: He is a mighty mind, but lost in contradictions.

*Zamora*: A wondrous harp strung in no key we know

*Himbal*: A vagrant word seeking a friendly ear.

# CHAPTER SEVEN

# Micayon and Naronda
## Hold a Nocturnal Chat with Mirdad
## Who Hints to Them of the Coming Flood
## and Bids Them to be Ready

*Naronda*: It was about the second hour of the third watch when I felt my cell door open and heard Micayon speaking to me at low breath,

'Are you awake, Naronda?'

'Sleep has not visited my cell this night, Micayon.'

'Nor has it nestled in my eyelids, And *he* – think you he sleeps?'

'Mean you the Master?'

'Call you him Master already? Mayhap he is. I cannot rest till I make sure of his identity. Let us to him this very minute.'

We tiptoed out of my cell and into that of the Master. A sheaf of paling moonlight, stealing through an aperture high up in the wall, fell on his humble bedding which was neatly spread on the floor and quite evidently untouched that night. He whom we sought was not to be found where we sought him.

Puzzled, ashamed and disappointed, we were about to retrace our steps when, of a sudden, his gentle voice reached our ears before our eyes could glimpse his gracious countenance at the door.

MIRDAD: Be not perturbed, and sit you down in peace. Night on the peaks is fast dissolving into dawn.

The hour is propitious for dissolving.

*Micayon*: (Perplexed and stammering) Forgive our intrusion. We have not slept all night.

MIRDAD: Too brief a self-forgetfulness is sleep. Better it is to drown the self, awake, than sip forgetfulness by thimblefuls of sleep. What seek you of Mirdad?

*Micayon*: We came to find out who you are.

MIRDAD: When with men, I am a god. When with God, I am a man. Have you found out, Micayon?

*Micayon*: You speak a blasphemy.

50

MIRDAD: Against Micayon's God – perhaps. Against the God of Mirdad – never.

*Micayon*: Are there as many gods as men that you should speak of one for Micayon and another for Mirdad?

MIRDAD: God is not many. God is one. But many and divers are yet men's shadows. So long as men cast shadows on the earth, so long is each man's god no greater than his shadow. The shadowless only are all in the light. The shadowless only know one God. For God is Light, and Light alone is able to know Light.

*Micayon*: Speak not to us in riddles. Too feeble yet is our understanding.

MIRDAD: All is a riddle to the man who trails a shadow. For that man walks in borrowed light, therefore he stumbles on his shadow. When you become ablaze with Understanding, then shall you cast no shadows any more.

Yet before long Mirdad shall gather up your shadows and burn them in the Sun. Then that which is a riddle to you now shall burst upon you as a blazing truth too evident to need expounding.

*Micayon*: Would you not tell us who you are? Perhaps, if we knew your name – your real name – your country and your ancestry we would the better understand you.

MIRDAD: Ah, Micayon! As well force an eagle back into the shell out of which he hatched as try to chain Mirdad with your chains and veil him in your veils. What name can ever designate a Man who is no longer 'in the shell'? What country can contain a Man in whom an universe is contained? What ancestry can claim a Man whose only ancestor is God?

If you would know me well, Micayon, first know Micayon well.

*Micayon*: Perhaps you are a myth wearing the garb of man.

MIRDAD: Aye, people shall say some day, Mirdad was but a myth. But you shall know anon how *real* is this myth – how more real than any kind of men's reality.

The world is now unmindful of Mirdad. Mirdad is ever mindful of the world. The world shall soon be mindful of Mirdad.

*Micayon*: Are you, perchance, the Stowaway?

MIRDAD: I am the stowaway in every ark breasting the deluge of delusion. I take the helm whenever captains call on me for help. Your hearts, although you know it not, have called aloud to me since long ago. And, lo! Mirdad is here to steer you safely on that you, in turn, may steer the world out of the greatest deluge ever known.

*Micayon*: Another flood?

MIRDAD: Not to wash out the Earth, but to bring out the heaven in the Earth. Not to efface the trace of Man, but to uncover God in Man.

*Micayon*: The rainbow graded our skies but a few days agone. How speak you of another flood?

MIRDAD: More devastating than the flood of Noah shall be the flood already raging on.

An earth engulfed in waters is an earth pregnant with promises of Spring. Not so an earth a-stew in her own feverish blood.

*Micayon*: Are we to look, then, for the end? For we are told that the coming of the Stowaway shall be the signal of the end.

MIRDAD: Have no fear for the Earth. Too young is she, and too overflowing are her breasts. More generations shall she suckle yet than you can count.

Nor have anxiety for Man, the master of the Earth, for he is indestructible.

Yea, ineffaceable is Man. Yea, inexhaustible is Man. He shall go into the forge a man but shall emerge a god.

Be steady. Make ready. Keep your eyes, and ears, and tongues on fast so that your hearts may know that holy hunger which, once appeased, leaves you forever full.

You must be ever-full that you may fill the wanting. You must be ever strong and steady that you may prop the wavering and the weak. You must be ever ready for the storm that you may shelter all the storm-tossed waifs. You must be ever luminous that you may guide the walkers in the dark.

The weak are burdens to the weak. But to the strong they are a pleasant charge. Seek out the weak. Their weakness is your strength

The hungry are but hunger to the hungry. But to the full they are a welcome outlet. Seek out the hungry. Your fulness is their want.

The blind are stumbling-blocks to the blind. But they are mile-posts to the seeing. Seek out the blind. Their darkness is your light.

*Naronda*: At this point the trumpet sounded forth the call to morning prayer.

MIRDAD: Zamora trumpets in another day – another miracle for you to yawn away between down-sittings and uprisings, charging your stomachs and discharging them, whetting your tongues with idle words, and doing many deeds which were better undone, and not doing the deeds which need be done.

*Micayon*: Shall we not go to prayer, then?

MIRDAD: Go! Pray as you have been taught to pray. Pray anyway – for anything. Go! Do all the things commanded you to do till you become self-taught and self-commanded, and till you learn to make each word a prayer, each deed a sacrifice. Go in peace. Mirdad must see that your morning meal be plentiful and sweet.

# CHAPTER EIGHT

# The Seven seek Mirdad in the Aerie
## where he warns them
## of doing things in the dark

*Naronda*: That day Micayon and I went not to morning devotions. Shamadam noted our absence and, having learned of our night visit to the Master, was sore displeased. Yet he vented not his displeasure, biding another time.

The rest of the companions were much aroused by our behaviour and wished to know thereof the reason. Some thought it was the Master who counselled us against praying. Others made curious conjectures as to his identity saying that he had called us unto him at night in order to reveal himself to us alone. None would believe he was the Stowaway. But all desired to see him and to question him on many things.

It was the Master's wont, when free from duties in the Ark, to spend his hours in the grotto overhanging the Black Pit, which grotto was known among us as the Aerie. We sought him there, all of us save Shamadam, the afternoon of that day, and found him deep in meditation. His face was aglow, and it glowed brighter when he lifted up his eyes and saw us.

MIRDAD: How quickly you have found your nest. Mirdad is joyful for your sakes.

*Abimar*: The Ark is our nest. How say you, this grotto is our nest?

MIRDAD: The Ark was once an Aerie.

*Abimar*: And to-day?

MIRDAD: A mole burrow, alas!

*Abimar*: Eight happy moles with Mirdad as the ninth!

MIRDAD: How easy it is to mock; how hard to understand!

Yet mockery has ever mocked the mocker. Why exercise your tongue in vain?

*Abimar*: 'Tis you that mock us when you call us moles. Wherein have we deserved of such an appellation? Have we not kept the fire of Noah burning? This Ark, once a hovel for a handful of beggars, have we not made it richer than the richest palace? Have we not thrust its borders far till it became a mighty kingdom? If we be moles, then are we master burrowers, indeed.

MIRDAD: The fire of Noah burns, but only on the altar. Of what avail is it to you except you be the altar, and your hearts the fire-wood and the oil?

The Ark is overcharged with gold and silver now; therefore it squeaks and pitches hard and is about to founder. Whereas the mother-ark was overcharged with Life and carried no dead weight; therefore the deeps were powerless against it.

Beware of dead weight, my companions. All is a dead weight to the man who has a firm faith in his godhood. He holds in himself the world, yet carries not its weight.

I say to you, except you jettison your silver and your gold they'll drag you with them to the bottom. For Man is held by everything he holds. Release your grip on things if you would not be in their grip.

Set not on anything a price, for the slightest thing is priceless. You price a loaf of bread. Why not price the Sun, the Air, the Earth, the Sea and the sweat and ingenuity of Man without which there could have been no loaf?

Set not on anything a price lest you be setting prices on your lives. No dearer is Man's life than that which he holds dear. Take care that you hold not your priceless life so cheap as gold.

The borders of the Ark you thrust for leagues away. Were you to thrust them to the borders of the Earth, you would still be hemmed in and confined. Mirdad would have you belt and cap infinity. The sea is but an earth-held drop, yet does it belt and cap the earth. How much more infinite a sea is Man? Be not so childish as to measure him from head to foot and think that you have found his borders.

You may be master-burrowers, as Abimar has said; but only as the mole that labours in the dark. The more elaborate his labyrinths, the further from the Sun his face. I know your labyrinths, Abimar. You are a handful, as you say; supposedly divorced from all the world's temptations and consecrated unto God. Yet devious and dark are the paths that link you with the world. Do I not hear your passions hiss and toss? Do I not see your envies crawl and writhe upon the very altar of your God? A handful you may be. But, Oh, what legions in that handful!

Were you, in very deed, the master-burrowers you say you are, you should have long since burrowed your way not only through the earth, but through the sun as well and every other sphere a-whirl in the firmament.

Let moles burrow their dark pathways with snout and paw. You need not move an eyelash to find your royal road. Sit in this nest and send Imagination forth. He is your guide divine unto the wondrous treasures of the trackless being which is your kingdom. Follow your guide with stout and fearless hearts. His footprints, be they in the farthest star, shall be to you as signs and sureties that you have already been planted there. For you cannot imagine aught save it be in you or a part of you.

A tree can spread no further than its roots. While Man can spread unto infinity, for he is rooted in eternity.

Set no limits to yourselves. Spread out until there are no regions where you are not. Spread out until the whole world be wherever you may chance to be. Spread out till you meet God where'er you meet yourselves. Spread out. Spread out!

Do nothing in the dark in the belief that darkness is a cover impenetrable. If you be unashamed of darkness-blinded men, have shame, at least, of the firefly and the bat.

There is no darkness, my companions. There are degrees of light so graduated as to meet the need of every creature in the world. Your broad day is twilight to the phoenix. Your deep night is broad day to the frog. If darkness itself be uncovered, how can it be for anything a cover?

Seek not to cover anything at all. If naught reveal your secrets, their very cover will. Does not the lid know what is in the pot? Woe to the snake-and-worm-filled pots when their lids are lifted.

I say to you, no breath escapes your breasts except it broadcast on wind the innermost of your breasts. No glance is shot from any eye except it carry with it all the eye, its lusts and fears, its smiles and tears. No dream has ever entered any door except it knocked at every other door. Take care, then, how you look. Take care what dreams you let in the door and what you let go by.

If you, however, would be free of care and pain, Mirdad would fain point out the way.

# CHAPTER NINE

## The Way to Painless Life.
## Companions would Know
## if Mirdad be the Stowaway

*Micaster:* Show us the way.

MIRDAD: This is the way to freedom from care and pain:

*So think as if your every thought were to be etched in fire upon the sky for all and everything to see. For so, in truth, it is.*

*So speak as if the world entire were but a single ear intent on hearing what you say. And so, in truth, it is.*

*So do as if your every deed were to recoil upon your heads. And so, in truth, it does.*

*So wish as if you were the wish. And so, in truth, you are.*

*So live as if your God Himself had need of you His life to live. And so, in truth, He does.*

*Himbal:* How much longer shall you keep us puzzled? You speak to us as no man, and no book ever spoke.

*Bennoon:* Declare yourself that we may know what ear to hear you with. If you be the Stowaway, give us some proof.

MIRDAD: Well have you said, Bennoon, You have too many ears; therefore you cannot hear. Had you but one that heard and understood, you would require no proof.

*Bennoon:* The Stowaway should come to judge the world, and we of the Ark should sit with him in judgment. Shall we make ready for the Judgment Day?

# CHAPTER TEN

# On Judgment and the Judgment Day

MIRDAD: There is no judgment in my mouth, but Holy Understanding. I am not come to judge the world, but rather to unjudge it. For Ignorance alone likes to be decked in wig and robe and to propound the law and mete out penalties.

The most unsparing judge of Ignorance is Ignorance itself. Consider Man. Has he not, in ignorance, cloven himself in twain thereby inviting death upon himself and all the things that make up his divided world?

I say to you, there is not God *and* Man. But there is God-Man or Man-God. There is the One. However multiplied, however divided, it is forever One.

God's oneness is God's everlasting law. It is a self-enforcing law. Nor courts nor judges does it need to publish it abroad or to uphold its dignity and force. The Universe – the visible of it and the invisible – is but a single mouth proclaiming it to all who have but ears to hear.

Is not the Sea – though vast and deep – a single drop?

Is not the Earth – though flung so far – a single sphere?

Are not the spheres – though numberless – a single universe?

Likewise is mankind but a single Man. Likewise is Man, with all his worlds, a singleness complete.

God's oneness, my companions, is the only law of being. Another name for it is Love. To know it and abide by it is to abide in Life. But to abide by any other law is to abide in non-being, or Death.

Life is a gathering in. Death is a scattering out. Life is a binding together. Death is a falling away. Therefore is Man – the dualist – suspended 'twixt the two. For he would gather in, but only through scattering out. And he would bind, but only by unbinding. In gathering and binding he is in keeping with The Law; and Life is his reward. In scattering and unbinding he sins against The Law; and Death is his bitter prize.

Yet you, the self-condemned, would sit in judgment over men

who are, like you, already self-condemned. How horrible the judges and the judgment!

Less horrible, indeed, would be two gallows-birds each sentencing the other to the gallows.

Less laughable two oxen in one yoke each saying to the other, 'I would yoke you'.

Less hideous two corpses in one grave exchanging condemnations to the grave.

Less pitiful two stone-blind men each plucking out the other's eyes.

Shun every judgment seat, my companions. For to pronounce a judgment on anyone, or anything, you must not only know The Law and live conformably thereto, but hear the evidence as well. Whom shall you hear as witnesses in any case at hand?

Shall you summon the wind into the court? For the wind aids and abets in any happening beneath the sky.

Or shall you cite the stars? For they are privy to all things that take place in the world?

Or shall you send subpoenae to the dead from Adam till this day? For all the dead are living in the living.

To have an evidence complete in any given case the Cosmos must needs be the witness. When you can hail the Cosmos into court, you would require no courts. You would descend from judgment seat and let the witness be the judge.

When you know all, you would judge none.

When you can gather in the worlds, you would condemn not even one of those who scatter out. For you would know that scattering condemned the scatterer. And rather than condemn the self-condemned, you would then strive to lift his condemnation.

Too overburdened now is Man with burdens self-imposed. Too rough and crooked is his road. Each judgment is an added burden, alike to the judge and the judged. If you would have your burdens light, refrain from judging any man. If you would have them vanish of themselves, sink and be lost forever in the Word. Let Understanding guide your steps if you would have your pathway straight and smooth.

Not judgment do I bring you in my mouth, but Holy Understanding.

*Bennoon*: What of the Judgment Day?

MIRDAD: Each day, Bennoon, is Judgment Day. Each creature's accounts are balanced every twinkling of an eye. Nothing is hid. Nothing is left unweighed.

There is no thought, no deed, no wish but are recorded in the thinker and the doer and the wisher. No thought, no wish, no deed go sterile in the world, but all beget after their kind and nature. Whatever is in keeping with God's Law is gathered unto Life. Whatever is opposed is gathered unto Death.

Your days are not alike, Bennoon. Some are serene. They are the harvestings of hours rightly lived.

Some are beset with clouds. They are the gifts of hours half-asleep in Death and half-awake in Life.

While others dash on you astride a storm, with lightning in their eyes, and thunder in their nostrils. They smite you from above; they whip you from below; they toss you right and left; they flatten you onto the earth and make you bite the dust and wish you were never born. Such days are the fruit of hours spent in wilful opposition to The Law.

So is it with the world. The shadows already athwart the skies are not a whit less ominous than those which ushered in the Flood. Open your eyes and see.

When you observe the clouds riding the South Wind northward, you say they bring you rain. Why are you not as wise in measuring the drift of human clouds? Can you not see how fast have men become entangled in their nets?

The day of disentangling is at hand. And what a fearful day it is!

With heart and soul-veins have the nets of men been woven over the course of, lo, so many centuries. To tear men free of their nets, their very flesh must needs be torn; their very bone must needs be crushed. And men themselves shall do the tearing and the crushing.

When the lids are lifted – as surely they shall be – and when the pots give out whatever they contain – as surely they shall do – where would men hide their shame, and whither would they flee?

In that day the living shall have envy of the dead, and the dead shall curse the living. Men's words shall stick within their throats, and the light shall freeze upon their eyelids. Out of their hearts shall issue scorpions and vipers, and they shall cry in awe, 'Whence come these vipers and these scorpions?', forgetting that they lodged and reared them in their hearts.

Open your eyes and see. Right in this Ark, set as a beacon to a floundering world, there is more mire than you can muddle through. If the beacon have become a snare, how terrible must be the state of those at sea!

Mirdad will build you a new ark. Right in this nest shall he found it and rear it. Out of this nest shall you fly unto the world bearing not olive twigs to men, but Life inexhaustible. For that you must know The Law and keep it.

*Zamora*: How shall we know God's Law and keep it?

# CHAPTER ELEVEN

# Love is the Law of God
# Mirdad divines Estrangement
# Between Two Companions, calls for Harp
# and Sings Hymn of the New Ark

MIRDAD: Love is the Law of God.

You live that you may learn to love. You love that you may learn to live. No other lesson is required of Man.

And what is it to love but for the lover to absorb forever the beloved so that the twain be one?

And whom, or what, is one to love? Is one to choose a certain leaf upon the Tree of Life and pour upon it all one's heart? What of the branch that bears the leaf? What of the stem that holds the branch? What of the bark that shields the stem? What of the roots that feed the bark, the stem, the branches and the leaves? What of the soil embosoming the roots? What of the sun, and sea, and air that fertilize the soil?

If one small leaf upon a tree be worthy of your love how much more so the tree in its entirety? The love that singles out a fraction of the whole foredooms itself to grief.

You say, 'But there be leaves and leaves upon a single tree. Some are healthy, some are sick; some are beautiful, some, ugly; some are giants, some are dwarfs. How can we help but pick and choose?'

I say to you, Out of the paleness of the sick proceeds the freshness of the healthy. I further say to you that ugliness is Beauty's palette, paint and brush; and that the dwarf would not have been a dwarf had he not given of his stature to the giant.

You are the tree of Life. Beware of fractioning yourselves. Set not a fruit against a fruit, a leaf against a leaf, a bough against a bough; nor set the stem against the roots; nor set the tree against the mother-soil. That is precisely what you do when you love one part more than the rest, or to the exclusion of the rest.

You are the Tree of Life. Your roots are everywhere. Your boughs and leaves are everywhere. Your fruits are in every mouth. Whatever be the fruits upon that tree; whatever be its boughs and leaves;

whatever be its roots, they are your fruits; they are your leaves and boughs; they are your roots. If you would have the tree bear sweet and fragrant fruit, if you would have it ever strong and green, see to the sap wherewith you feed the roots.

Love is the sap of Life. While Hatred is the pus of Death. But Love, like blood, must circulate unhindered in the veins. Repress the blood, and it becomes a menace and a plague. And what is Hate but Love repressed, or Love withheld, therefore becoming such a deadly poison both to the feeder and the fed; both to the hater and to that he hates?

A yellow leaf upon your tree of life is but a Love-weaned leaf. Blame not the yellow leaf.

A withered bough is but a Love-starved bough. Blame not the withered bough.

A putrid fruit is but a Hatred-suckled fruit. Blame not the putrid fruit. But rather blame your blind and stingy heart that would dole out the sap of life to few and would deny it to many, thereby denying it to itself.

No love is possible except the love of self. No self is real save the All-embracing Self. Therefore is God all Love, because He loves Himself.

So long as you are pained by Love, you have not found your real self, nor have you found the golden key of Love. Because you love an ephemeral self, your love is ephemeral.

The love of man for woman is not love. It is thereof a very distant token. The love of parent for the child is but the threshold to Love's holy temple. Till every man be every woman's lover, and the reverse; till every child be every parent's child, and the reverse, let men and women brag of flesh and bone clinging to flesh and bone, but never speak the sacred name of Love. For that is blasphemy.

You have no friends so long as you can count a single man as foe. The heart that harbours enmity how can it be a safe abode for friendship?

You do not know the joy of Love so long as there is hatred in your hearts. Were you to feed all things the sap of Life except a certain tiny worm, that certain tiny worm alone would embitter your life. For in loving anything, or anyone, you love in truth but yourselves. Likewise in hating anything, or anyone, you hate in truth but yourselves. For that which you hate is bound up inseparably with that which you love, like the face and the reverse of the same coin, If you would be honest with yourselves, then must you love what you hate and what hates you before you love what you love and what loves you.

Love is not a virtue. Love is a necessity; more so than bread and water; more so than light and air.

Let no one pride himself on loving. But rather breathe in Love and breathe it out just as unconsciously and freely as you breathe in the air and breathe it out.

For Love needs no one to exalt it. Love will exalt the heart that it finds worthy of itself.

Seek no rewards for Love. Love is reward sufficient unto Love, as Hate is punishment sufficient unto Hate.

Nor keep any accounts with Love. For Love accounts to no one but itself.

Love neither lends nor borrows; Love neither buys nor sells; but when it gives, it gives its all; and when it takes, it takes its all. Its very taking is a giving. Its very giving is a taking. Therefore is it the same to-day, to-morrow and forevermore.

Just as a mighty river emptying itself in the sea is e'er replenished by the sea, so must you empty yourselves in Love that you may be ever filled with Love. The pool that would withhold the sea-gift from the sea becomes a stagnant pool.

There is nor 'more' nor 'less' in Love. The moment you attempt to grade and measure Love it slips away leaving behind it bitter memories.

Nor is there 'now' and 'then', nor 'here' and 'there' in Love. All seasons are Love seasons. All spots are fit abodes for Love.

Love knows no boundaries or bars. A love whose course is checked by any obstacle whatever is not yet worthy of the name of Love.

I often hear you say that Love is blind, meaning that it can see no fault in the beloved. That kind of blindness is the height of seeing.

Would you were always so blind as to behold no fault in anything.

Nay, clear and penetrating is the eye of Love. Therefore it sees no fault. When Love has purged your sight, then would you see nothing at all unworthy of your love. Only a love-shorn, faulty eye is ever busy finding faults. Whatever faults it finds are only its own faults.

Love integrates. Hatred disintegrates. This huge and ponderous mass of earth and rock which you call Altar Peak would quickly fly asunder were it not held together by the hand of Love. Even your bodies, perishable as they seem, could certainly resist disintegration did you but love each cell of them with equal zeal.

Love is peace athrob with melodies of Life. Hatred is war agog with fiendish blasts of Death. Which would you: Love and be at everlasting peace? Or hate and be at everlasting war?

The whole earth is alive in you. The heavens and their hosts are alive in you. So love the Earth and all her sucklings if you would love yourselves. And love the Heavens and all their tenants if you would love yourselves.

Why do you hate Naronda, Abimar?

*Naronda*: All were taken aback by so sudden a shift in the Master's voice and course of thought; while Abimar and I were dumb-struck by so pointed a question about an estrangement between us which we carefully hid from all and had reasons to believe it was not detected by any. All looked upon the two of us in utter wonder and waited on the lips of Abimar.

*Abimar*: (Eying me in reproach) Did you, Naronda, tell the Master?

*Naronda*: When Abimar has said 'The Master', my heart melted in joy within me. For it was round that word that we had disagreed long before Mirdad revealed himself; I holding that he was a teacher come to enlighten men; and Abimar insisting, he was but a common man.

MIRDAD: Look not askance upon Naronda, Abimar; for he is blameless of your blame.

*Abimar*: Who told you, then? Can you read men's minds too?

MIRDAD: Mirdad needs nor spies nor interpreters. Did you but love Mirdad as he loves you, you could with ease read in his mind and see into his heart as well.

*Abimar*: Forgive a blind and a deaf man, Master. Open my eye and ear, for I am eager to see and to hear.

MIRDAD: Love is the only wonder-worker. If you would see let

Love be in the pupil of the eye. If you would hear, let Love be in the drum of the ear.

*Abimar*: But I hate no man, not even Naronda.

MIRDAD: Not-hating is not loving, Abimar. For Love is an active force; and save it guide your every move and step, you cannot find your way; and save it fill your every wish and thought, your wishes shall be nettles in your dreams; your thoughts shall be as dirges for your days.

Now is my heart a harp, and I am moved to song. Where is your harp, good Zamora?

*Zamora*: Shall I go and fetch it, Master?

MIRDAD: Go, Zamora.

*Naronda*: Zamora instantly arose and went for the harp. The rest looked at each other in utter bewilderment and held their peace.

When Zamora returned with the harp the Master gently took it from his hand, and bending over it in tenderness, carefully adjusted every string and then began to play and sing.

MIRDAD:

> God is your captain, sail, my Ark!
> Though Hell unleash her furies red
> Upon the living and the dead,
> And turn the earth to molten lead,
> And sweep the skies of every mark,
> God is your captain, sail, my Ark!

> Love is your compass, ply, my Ark!
> Go north and south, go east and west
> And share with all your treasure chest.
> The storm shall bear you on its crest
> A light for sailors in the dark.
> Love is your compass, ply, my Ark!

> Faith is your anchor, ride, my Ark!
> Should thunder roar, and lightning dart,
> And mountains shake and fall apart,
> And men become so faint of heart
> As to forget the holy spark,
> Faith is your anchor, ride, my Ark!

## Love is the Law of God

*Naronda*: The Master ceased and bent over the harp as bends a mother, love-entranced, over an infant at her breast. And though its strings no longer quivered, the harp continued to ring on, 'God is your captain, sail, my Ark!' And though the Master's lips were shut, his voice reverberated for a space throughout the Aerie and floated out in waves unto the rugged peaks about; unto the hills and vales below; unto the restless sea in the distance; unto the vaulted blue overhead.

There were star showers and rainbows in that voice. There were quakes and gales along with soughing winds and song-intoxicated nightingales. There were heaving seas empalled with soft, dew-laden mist. And it seemed as if the whole of creation were listening thereto in thankful gladness.

And it further seemed as if the Milky mountains range, with Altar Peak in the centre, had suddenly become detached from the Earth and were afloat in space, majestic, powerful and certain of its course.

For three days thereafter the Master spoke no word to any man.

# CHAPTER TWELVE

# On Creative Silence
## Speech is at best an Honest Lie

*Naronda:* When the three days were spent the Seven, as if by some irresistible command, gathered themselves together and made for the Aerie. The Master greeted us as one fully expecting our coming.

MIRDAD: Once more I welcome you, my fledglings, to your nest. Speak out your thoughts and wishes to Mirdad.

*Micayon:* Our only thought and wish is to be near Mirdad so we can feel and hear his truth, perchance we shall become as shadowless as he. His silence, howbeit, awes us all. Have we offended him in any way?

MIRDAD: Not to exile you from myself have I kept silent for three days; rather to draw you nearer to myself. As to offending me, whoever knows the peace invincible of Silence, the same can never be offended, nor offend.

*Micayon:* Is to be silent better than to speak?

MIRDAD: Speech is at best an honest lie. While silence is at worst a naked verity.

*Abimar:* Shall we conclude that even Mirdad's words, though honest, are but lies?

MIRDAD: Aye, even Mirdad's words are but lies to all whose *I* is not the same as Mirdad's. Till all your thoughts be quarried from one quarry, and all desires drawn of the selfsame well, your words, though honest, shall be lies.

When your *I* and mine are one, even as mine and God's are one, we would dispense with words and perfectly commune in truthful Silence.

Because your *I* and mine are not the same, I am constrained to wage on you a war of words that I may vanquish you with your own weapons and lead you to my quarry and my well.

And only then shall you be able to go forth into the world and vanquish and subdue it even as I shall vanquish and subdue you. And only then shall you be fit to lead the world unto the silence of the Consciousness Supreme, unto the quarry of the Word, unto the well of Holy Understanding.

Not till you be so vanquished by Mirdad shall you become in truth impregnable and mighty conquerors. Nor shall the world wash off the ignominy of its continuous defeat save when defeated by you.

So gird yourselves for battle. Furbish your shields and breast-plates, and whet your swords and spears. Let Silence beat the drum and bear the standard too.

*Bennoon*: What manner of Silence is this that should be at once the drummer and the standard-bearer?

MIRDAD: The silence I would usher you into is that interminable expanse wherein non-being passes into being, and being into non-being. It is that awesome void where every sound is born and hushed and every form is shaped and crushed; where every self is writ and unwrit; where nothing is but IT.

Except you cross that void and that expanse in silent contemplation, you shall not know how real is your being, how unreal the non-being. Nor shall you know how fast your reality is bound up with all Reality.

It is that Silence I would have you roam, that you may shed your old tight skin and move about unfettered, unrestrained.

It is there I would have you drive your cares and fears, your passions and desires, your envies and your lusts that you may see them vanish one by one and thus relieve your ears of their incessant cries, and spare your sides the pain of their sharp spurs.

It is there I would have you fling the bows and arrows of this world wherewith you hope to hunt contentment and joy, yet hunt in truth nothing but restlessness and sorrow.

It is there I would have you crawl out of the dark and stifling shell of self into the light and free air of The Self.

This Silence I commend unto you and not a mere respite for your speechworn tongues.

The fruitful silence of the Earth do I commend unto you, and not the fearful silence of the felon and the knave.

The patient silence of the setting hen do I commend unto you, not the impatient cackling of her laying sister. The one sets on for one and twenty days and waits in silent confidence upon the Mystic Hand to bring about the miracle beneath her downy breast and wings. The other darts out of her coop and madly cackles on announcing her deliverance of an egg.

Beware of cackling virtue, my companions. As you muzzle your shame, so muzzle your honour too. For a cackling honour is worse than a silent dishonour; and clamorous virtue is worse than dumb iniquity.

Refrain from speaking much. Out of a thousand words uttered there may be one, and one only, that need in truth be uttered. The rest but cloud the mind, and stuff the ear, and irk the tongue, and blind the heart as well.

How hard it is to say the word that need in truth be said!

Out of a thousand words written there may be one, and one only, that need in truth be written. The rest are wasted ink and paper, and minutes given feet of lead instead of wings of light.

How hard, Oh, how hard it is to write the word that need in truth be written!

*Bennoon:* What of prayer, Master Mirdad? In praying we are made to say too many words and ask for far too many things. Yet seldom are we granted any of the things we ask for.

# CHAPTER THIRTEEN
## On Prayer

MIRDAD: You pray in vain when you address yourselves to any other gods but your very selves.

For in you is the power to attract, as in you is the power to repel.

And in you are the things you would attract, as in you are the things you would repel.

For to be able to receive a thing is to be able to bestow it also.

Where there is hunger, there is food. Where there is food, there must be hunger too. To be afflicted with the pain of hunger is to be able to enjoy the blessing of being filled.

Yea, in the want is the supply of want.

Is not the key a warrant for the lock? Is not the lock a warrant for the key? Are not both lock and key a warrant for the door?

Be not in haste to importune the smith each time you lose, or misplace any key. The smith has done his work, and he has done it well; and he must not be asked to do the same work over and again. Do you your work, and let the smith alone; for he, once done with you, has other business to attend. Remove the stench and rubbish from your memory, and you shall surely find the key.

When God the unutterable uttered you forth, He uttered forth Himself in you. Thus you, too, are unutterable.

No fraction of Himself did God endow you with – for He is infractionable; but with His godhood entire, indivisible, unspeakable did He endow you all. What greater heritage can you aspire to have? And who, or what, can hinder you from coming thereinto except your own timidity and blindness?

Yet rather than be grateful for their heritage, and rather than seek out the way of coming thereinto, some men – the blind ingrates! – would make of God a sort of dumping hole whither to cart their tooth and belly aches, their losses in a trade, their quarrels, their revenges and their insomnious nights.

While others would have God as their exclusive treasure-house where they expect to find at any time they wished whatever they did crave of all the tinselled trinkets of this world.

And others still would make of God a sort of personal bookkeeper. He must not only keep accounts of what they owe and what the others owe them, but must as well collect their debts and always show a fat and handsome balance in their favour.

Aye, many and divers are the tasks that men assign to God. Yet few men seem to think that if, indeed, God were so charged with many tasks, He would perform them all alone and would require no man to goad Him on, or to remind Him of his tasks.

Do you remind God of the hours for the sun to rise and for the moon to set?

Do you remind Him of the grain of corn springing to life in yonder field?

Do you remind Him of yon spider spinning his masterful retreat?

Do you remind Him of the fledglings in that sparrow's nest?

Do you remind Him of the countless things that fill this boundless universe?

Why do you press your puny selves with all your trifling needs upon His memory? Are you less favoured in His sight than sparrows, corn and spiders? Why do you not, as they, receive your gifts and go about your labours without ado, without knee-bending, arm-extending, and without peering anxiously into the morrow?

And where is God that you should shout into His ear your whims and vanities, your praises and your plaints? Is He not in you and all about you? Is not His ear much nearer to your mouth than is your tongue to your palate?

Sufficient unto God is His godhood of which you have the seed.

If God, having given you the seed of His godhood, were to attend it and not you, what virtue would you have? And what would be the labour of your life? And if you have no labour to perform, but God must perform it for you, of what account were, then, your life? Of what avail were all your praying?

Take not to God your countless cares and hopes. Implore Him not to open for you the doors whereto He furnished you with keys. But search the vastness of your hearts. For in the vastness of the heart is found the key to every door. And in the vastness of the heart are all the things you thirst and hunger after, whether of evil or of good.

A mighty host is placed at your beck and call ready to do your slightest bidding. When properly equipped, and wisely disciplined, and fearlessly commanded it can be made to leap eternities and sweep away all barriers to its goal. When malequipped, undisciplined and timidly commanded it either churns about, or hastily retreats before the smallest obstacle, trailing behind it black defeat.

No other is that host, O monks, than those minute red corpuscles now silently coursing through your veins; each one of them a miracle of strength, each one a full and honest record of all your life and of all Life in its most intimate details.

In the heart does this host assemble; from the heart does it deploy. Hence is the heart so famed and so revered. Out of it gush your tears of joy and sorrow. Into it rush your fears of Life and Death.

Your cravings and desires are the equipment of this host. Your Mind is thereof the disciplinarian. Your Will, the driller and commander.

When you are able to equip your blood with one Master-Desire that silences and overshadows all desires; and trust one Master-Thought with the discipline; and charge one Master-Will with drilling and commanding, then certain you may be of that desire's fulfilment.

How does a saint attain to saintliness except by purging his bloodstream of every wish and thought incongruous to saintliness, and then directing it with an unwavering will to seek no other end but saintliness?

I say to you that every saintly wish, and every saintly thought, and every saintly will, from Adam till this day, will rush to aid the man so bent on reaching saintliness. For ever has it been that waters anywhere will seek the sea, as rays of light will seek the sun.

How does a murderer accomplish his designs except by whipping up his blood into a frenzied thirst for murder, and marshalling its cells in serried ranks under the lash of murder-mastered thought, and then commanding it with a relentless will to strike the fatal blow?

I say to you that every murderer, from Cain until this day, will rush unasked to strengthen and to steady that man's arm who is so drunk with murder. For ever has it been that ravens anywhere will consort with ravens, and hyenas with hyenas.

To pray, therefore, is to infuse the blood with one Master-Desire, one Master-Thought, one Master-Will. It is so to attune the self as to become in perfect harmony with whatever you pray for.

This planet's atmosphere, mirrored in all details within your hearts, is billowing with vagrant memories of all the things it witnessed since its birth.

No word or deed; no wish or sigh; no passing thought or transient dream; no breath of man or beast; no shadow, no illusion but ply in it their mystic courses till this very day, and shall so ply them to the end of Time. Attune your heart to anyone of these, and it shall surely dash to play upon the strings.

You need no lip or tongue for praying. But rather do you need a silent, wakeful heart, a Master-Wish, a Master-Thought, and above all, a Master-Will that neither doubts nor hesitates. For words are of no avail except the heart be present and awake in every syllable. And when the heart is present and awake, the tongue had better go to sleep, or hide behind sealed lips.

Nor have you any need of temples to pray in.

Whoever cannot find a temple in his heart, the same can never find his heart in any temple.

Yet this I say to you and to the ones like you, but not to every man. For most men are derelict as yet. They feel the need of praying, but know not the way. They cannot pray except with words, and they can find no words except you put them in their mouths. And they are lost and awed when made to roam the vastness of their hearts, but soothed and comforted within the walls of temples and in the herds of creatures like themselves.

Let them erect their temples. Let them chant out their prayers.

But you and every man I charge to pray for Understanding. To hunger after anything but that is never to be filled.

Remember that the key to Life is the Creative Word. The key to the Creative Word is Love. The key to Love is Understanding. Fill up your hearts with these and spare your tongues the pain of many words, and save your minds the weight of many prayers, and free your hearts from bondage to all gods who would enslave you with a gift; who would caress you with one hand only to smite you with the other; who are content and kindly when you praise them, but wrathful and revengeful when reproached; who would not hear you save you call, and would not give you save you beg; and having given you, too oft regret the giving; whose incense is your tear; whose glory is your shame.

Aye, free your hearts of all these gods that you may find in them the only God who, having filled you with Himself, would have you ever full.

*Bennoon*: Now you speak of Man as omnipotent; now you belittle him as a derelict. You leave us in fog, as it were.

# CHAPTER FOURTEEN

# The Colloquy between Two Archangels, and the Colloquy between Two Archdemons at the Timeless Birth of Man

MIRDAD: At the timeless birth of Man two archangels at the upper pole of the Universe held the following colloquy:

Said the first archangel:

A wondrous child has been born unto Earth; and Earth is ablaze with light.

Said the second archangel:

A glorious king has been born unto Heaven; and Heaven is athrob with joy.

1st: He is the fruit of the union 'twixt Heaven and Earth.

2nd: He is the union eternal – the father, the mother and the child.

1st: In him is Earth exalted.

2nd: In him is Heaven justified.

1st: Day is asleep in his eyes.

2nd: Night is awake in his heart.

1st: His breast is a nest of gales.

2nd: His throat is a scale of song.

1st: His arms embrace the mountains.

2nd: His fingers pluck the stars.

1st: Seas are roaring in his bones.

2nd: Suns are coursing in his veins.

1st: A forge and a mould is his mouth.

2nd: A hammer and an anvil his tongue.

1st: Round his feet are the chains of To-morrow.

2nd: In his heart is the key to the chains.

1st: Yet cradled in dust is this babe.

2nd: But swaddled in aeons is he.

1st: Like God does he hold of numbers every secret. Like God does he know the mystery of words.

2nd: All numbers does he know but the Sacred One, which is the first and last. All words does he ken, save the Creative Word, which is the first and last.

1st: Yet shall he know the Number and the Word.

2nd: Not till he walks his feet away over the trackless wastes of Space; nor till he looks his eyes away upon the dismal vaults of Time.

1st: O wondrous, too wondrous is this child of Earth.

2nd: O glorious, too glorious is this king of Heaven.

1st: The Nameless called him Man.

2nd: And he called The Nameless God.

1st: Man is the word of God.

2nd: God is the word of Man.

1st: Glory to Him Whose word is Man.

2nd: Glory to him whose word is God.

1st: Now and forever.

2nd: Here and everywhere.

So spoke the two archangels at the upper pole of the Universe at the timeless birth of Man.

At the same time two archdemons at the nether pole of the Universe were holding the following colloquy:

Said the first archdemon:

A valiant warrior has joined our ranks. With his aid we shall conquer.

Said the second archdemon:

A whining and a snivelling coward, rather say. And treason is encamped on his brow. Yet terrible is he in his cowardice and treason.

1st: Fearless and wild is his eye.

2nd: Tearful and tame is his heart. Yet fearful is he in his tameness and tears.

1st: Keen and persistent is his mind.

2nd: Slothful and dull is his ear. Yet dangerous is he in his sloth and his dullness.

1st: Swift and precise is his hand.

2nd: Hesitant and sluggish is his foot. Yet dreadful is his sluggishness, and alarming is his hesitance.

1st: Our bread shall be steel to his nerves. Our wine shall be fire to his blood.

2nd: Our bread-bins he shall stone us with. Our wine-jars he shall break upon our heads.

1st: His lust for our bread, and his thirst for our wine shall be his chariot in battle.

2nd: With hunger unappeasable, and thirst unquenchable he shall be made unconquerable and raise rebellion in our camp.

1st: But Death shall be the charioteer.

2nd: With Death as his charioteer he shall become immortal.

1st: Shall Death lead him to aught but Death?

2nd: Aye, so wearied shall be Death of his constant whining that he shall drive him in the end into the camp of Life.

1st: Shall Death be a traitor to Death?

2nd: Nay, Life shall be faithful to Life.

1st: His palate we shall tease with rare and delectable fruit.

2nd: Yet shall he long for fruit not grown upon this pole.

1st: His eyes and nose we shall entice with bright and fragrant flowers.

2nd: Yet shall his eye seek other flowers, and his nose another fragrance.

1st: And we shall haunt his ears with sweet but distant melodies.

2nd: Yet shall his ear be towards another choir.

1st: Fear shall enslave him to us.

2nd: Hope shall protect him from fear.

1st: Pain shall subdue him to us.

2nd: Faith shall deliver him of pain.

1st: We shall empall his sleep with puzzling dreams, and strew his wakefulness with enigmatic shadows.

2nd: His Fancy shall undo the puzzles and melt away the shadows.

1st: Withal we can count him as one of us.

2nd: Count him with us, if you wish; but count him as against us also.

1st: Can he at once be with us and against us?

2nd: He is a lonely warrior in the field. His only adversary is his shadow. As shifts the shadow, so the battle shifts. He is with us when his shadow is in front. He is against us when his shadow is behind.

1st: Shall we not keep him, then, with his back forever to the Sun?

2nd: But who shall keep the Sun forever at his back?

1st: A riddle is this warrior.

2nd: A riddle is this shadow.

## The Colloquy between Two Archdemons

1st: Hail to the lonely knight.
2nd: Hail to the lonely shadow.
1st: Hail to him when with us.
2nd: Hail to him when against us.
1st: Now and forever.
2nd: Here and everywhere.

So spoke two archdemons at the nether pole of the Universe at the timeless birth of Man.

# CHAPTER FIFTEEN

## Shamadam makes an Effort
## to put Mirdad out of the Ark.
## The Master speaks of Insulting
## and Being Insulted, and of Containing the World
## in  Holy Understanding

*Naronda:* Hardly had the Master finished when the Senior's bulky frame appeared at the entrance of the Aerie and seemed to shut out the air and light. And it flashed through my mind for the instant that the figure at the entrance was no other than one of the two archdemons of whom the Master had just told us.

The Senior's eyes struck fire, and his beard bristled as he advanced towards the Master and grabbed him by the arm attempting, evidently, to drag him out.

*Shamadam:* I have just heard the awful vomitings of your vile mind. Your mouth is a spout of poison. Your presence is an omen of ill. As Senior of this Ark I bid you out this very instant.

*Naronda:* The Master, though slight of structure, held his ground with perfect ease as if he were a giant and Shamadam, but a babe. His equanimity was astounding as he looked at Shamadam and said,

MIRDAD: He only has the power to bid out who has the power to bid in. Did you, Shamadam, bid me in?

*Shamadam:* It was your wretchedness that moved my heart with pity, and I allowed you in.

MIRDAD: It is my love, Shamadam, that was moved by your wretchedness. And lo, I'm here, and with me is my love. But you, alas, are neither here nor there. Your shadow only flits hither and yon. And I am come to gather up all shadows and burn them in the Sun.

*Shamadam:* I was the Senior of this Ark long before your breath began to pollute the air. How does your vile tongue say, I am not here?

MIRDAD: Before these mountains were I was, and I shall be long after they have crumpled into dust.

I am the Ark, the altar and the fire. Save you be sheltered in me, you shall remain a prey to the storm. And save you immolate yourselves before me, you shall not know immunity from the ever-sharpened knives of Death's innumerable butchers. And save my tender fire consume you, you shall be fuel to the cruel fire of Hell.

*Shamadam*: Did you all hear? Did you not hear? With me, companions. Let us cast this blaspheming imposter into the pit below.

*Naronda*: Again Shamadam dashed towards the Master and grabbed him by the arm wishing to drag him out. But the Master neither flinched nor budged; nor did any companion make the slightest move. After a trying pause Shamadam's head fell to his chest, and he slunk out of the Aerie mumbling as to himself, 'I am the Senior of this Ark. I shall assert my God-given authority.'

The Master mused for long and would not speak. But Zamora could not hold his peace.

*Zamora*: Shamadam has insulted our Master. What would you, Master, that we do with him. Command us, and we shall strike.

MIRDAD: Pray for Shamadam, my companions. That is all I would have you do with him. Pray that his eyes may be unveiled, and his shadow lifted.

As easy it is to attract the good as to attract the evil. As easy to be tuned to Love as to be tuned to Hate.

Out of the boundless Space; out of the vastness of your hearts draw blessings on the world. For everything that is a blessing to the world is to you a blessing.

Pray for the good of all the creatures. For every good of every creature is your good as well. Likewise the ill of every creature is your ill as well.

Are you not all as moving rungs in the infinite ladder of Being? Those who would mount to holy Freedom's sphere must mount perforce upon the others' shoulders. And they, in turn, must make their shoulders rungs for the others to mount upon.

What is Shamadam but a rung in the ladder of your being? Would you not have your ladder strong and safe? Attend, then, to every rung and keep it safe and strong.

What is Shamadam but a stone in the foundation of your life? And what are you but stones in his and every creature's edifice of life? See that Shamadam be a faultless stone if you would have your edifice entirely free of fault. Be faultless yourselves that those into whose lives you may be built may have their edifice without a fault.

Think you, you are equipped with no more than two eyes? I say to you that every seeing eye, whether on Earth, above it, or below it, is an extension of your eye. To the extent your neighbour's sight is clear, to that extent your sight is also clear. To the extent your neighbour's sight is dimmed, to that extent your sight is also dimmed.

In every blind man you are deprived of a pair of eyes that otherwise would reinforce your eyes. Preserve your neighbour's sight that you may see the clearer. Preserve your own that your neighbour may not stumble and block, perhaps, your very door.

Zamora thinks Shamadam has insulted me. How can Shamadam's ignorance ruffle my understanding?

A muddy brook can easily muddy another brook. But can a muddy brook muddy the sea? The sea shall gladly take the mud and spread it in its bed, and give the brook clear water in return.

You can defile, or sterilize, a square foot of the earth – perhaps a mile. Who can defile or sterilize the Earth? The earth accepts all men's and beasts' impurities and gives them in return sweet fruits and fragrant flowers, and grains and grasses in abundance.

A sword can surely wound the flesh. But can it wound the air, however keen of edge and strong the arm behind it?

It is the pride of mean and narrow self, begot of blind and lustful ignorance that can insult and be insulted, and would avenge the insult with an insult and wash away the filth with filth.

The pride-ridden and self-intoxicated world shall heap up injuries upon your heads. It shall unleash on you the blood-thirsty hounds of its tattered laws, its putrid creeds, and mouldy honours. It shall proclaim you enemies of order and agents of chaos and doom. It shall bestrew your roads with snares and shall bedeck your beds with nettles. It shall sow curses in your ears and spit contempt upon your faces.

Let not your hearts be faint. But like the Sea be broad and deep, and give a blessing unto him that gives you but a curse.

And like the Earth be generous and calm, and turn impurities of men's hearts into pure health and beauty.

And like the Air be free and supple. The sword that would wound you would finally tarnish and rust. The arm that would harm you would finally weary and halt.

The world, not knowing you, cannot contain you. Therefore shall it receive you with a snarl. But you, knowing the world, can contain it. Therefore must you allay its wrath with kindliness, and drown its calumny in loving Understanding.

And Understanding shall carry the day.

So taught I Noah.

So I teach you.

*Naronda*: Thereupon the Seven dispersed in silence. For we had come to know that every time the Master concluded with these words 'So taught I Noah', it was a signal that he wished to speak no more.

# CHAPTER SIXTEEN

## On Creditors and Debtors.
## What is Money?
## Rustidion acquitted of his Debt to the Ark

*Naronda:* One day as the Seven and the Master were returning from the Aerie to the Ark they saw Shamadam at the gate waving a piece of paper at a man prostrated at his feet, and heard him saying in an angry voice: 'Your delinquency exhausts my patience. I can be lenient no longer. Pay now, or rot in prison.'

The man we recognized as Rustidion, one of the many tenants of the Ark who was indebted to the Ark for a certain sum of money. He was bent as much with rags as with years; and he pleaded with the Senior for time to pay the interest, saying that he had recently lost his only son and his only cow in the same week, and that his old wife, as a consequence, was struck with palsy. But Shamadam's heart would not soften.

The Master walked towards Rustidion and, taking him gently by the arm, he said,

MIRDAD: Arise, my Rustidion. You, too, are an image of God, and God's image must not be made to bow before any shadow. (Then turning to Shamadam)

Show me the bill of indebtedness.

*Naronda:* Shamadam, so furious but a moment before, became to the amazement of all more docile than a lamb, and meekly handed to the Master the paper in his hand, which paper the Master took and scrutinized for long with Shamadam bluntly looking on and saying nothing, as if in a spell.

MIRDAD: No money lender was the founder of this Ark. Did he bequeath you money to lend out with usury? Did he bequeath you chattels to trade in, or lands to rent and hoard the fat thereof? Did he bequeath you your brother's sweat and blood and then bequeath you prisons for the ones whose sweat you have drained to the end, whose blood you have sucked to a drop?

An Ark, and an altar, and a light did he bequeath you – nothing more. An ark which is his living body. An altar which is his dauntless

84

heart. A light which is his burning faith. And these he commanded you to keep intact and pure amid a world dancing to pipes of Death and wallowing in quagmires of iniquity, because of faithlessness.

And that the cares of the body may not distract your spirit, you were allowed to live upon the charity of the faithful. And never since the Ark was launched was there a dearth of charity.

But, lo! This charity have you now turned into a curse, both for yourselves and for the charitable. For with their gifts you subjugate the givers. You scourge them with the very thread they spin for you. You strip them naked with the very cloth they weave for you. You starve them with the very bread they bake for you. You build them prisons with the very stones they cut and dress for you. You fashion yokes and coffins for them out of the very wood they provide you for your warmth. Their very sweat and blood you loan them back with usury.

For what were money but the sweat and blood of men coined by the crafty into mites and shekels wherewith to shackle men? And what were riches but the sweat and blood of men garnered by those who sweat and bleed the least to grind therewith the backs of those who sweat and bleed the most?

Woe and woe again unto them who burn away their minds and hearts and slay their nights and days in storing riches! For they know not what they store.

The sweat of harlots, murderers and thieves; the sweat of the consumptive, the leper and the palsied; the sweat of the blind, and the halt, and the maimed with that of the ploughman and his ox, and of the shepherd and his sheep, and of the reaper and the gleaner – all these and many more do the storers of riches store.

The blood of the orphan and the rogue; of the despot and the martyr; of the wicked and the just; of the robber and the robbed; the blood of executioners and those they execute; the blood of leeches and cheats and those they suck and cheat – all these and many more do the storers of riches store.

Aye, woe and woe again to those whose riches and whose stock in trade is the sweat and blood of men! For sweat and blood will in the end exact their price. And terrible shall be the price, and fearful the exacting.

To lend, and lend with interest! That is indeed ingratitude too brazen to condone.

For what have you to lend? Is not your very life a gift? Were God to charge you interest for the least of His gifts unto you, wherewith would you pay?

Is not this world a common treasury wherein each man, each thing, deposit all they have for the maintenance of all?

Does the lark lend you its song, and the spring its sparkling water?

Does the oak loan its shade, and the palm its honeyed dates?

Does the sheep give you his wool, and the cow her milk for interest?

Do the clouds sell you their rain, and the Sun his warmth and light?

What would be your life without these things and myriad other things? And who of you can tell which man, which thing, have deposited the most, and which, the least in the treasury of the world?

Can you, Shamadam, calculate Rustidion's contributions to the treasury of the Ark? Yet would you lend him back his very contributions – perhaps but a trifling part thereof – and charge him interest to boot. Yet would you send him to prison and leave him there to rot?

What interest do you demand of Rustidion? Can you not see how profitable your loan has been to him? What better payment do you wish than a dead son, a dead cow and a palsied wife? What greater interest can you exact than these so mouldy rags upon so bent a back?

Ah, rub your eyes, Shamadam. Be awake before you, too, are asked to pay your debts with interest, and failing that, be dragged into prison and there be left to rot.

The same I say to all of you, companions. Rub your eyes, and be awake.

Give when you can, and all you can. But never lend, lest all you have, even your life, become a loan and the loan fall due at once, and you be found insolvent and cast into prison.

*Naronda*: The Master then looked again at the paper in his hand and deliberately tore it to shreds, which shreds he scattered to the wind. Then turning to Himbal, who was the keeper of the treasury, he said to him.

## On Creditors and Debtors

MIRDAD: Give Rustidion wherewith to buy two cows and care for his wife and himself to the end of their days.

And you, Rustidion, go in peace. You are acquitted of your debt. Take care that you never become a creditor. *For the debt of him who lends is greater and heavier by far than the debt of him who borrows.*

# CHAPTER SEVENTEEN

# Shamadam resorts to Bribery
# in his Fight against Mirdad

*Naronda*: For many days the case of Rustidion was the chief topic in the Ark. Micayon, Micaster and Zamora lauded the Master with vehemence, Zamora saying that he loathed the very sight and touch of money. Bennoon and Abimar mildly approved and disapproved. While Himbal openly disapproved saying that the world could never do without money, and that riches were God's just recompense of thrift and industry, as poverty was God's patent penalty of indolence and wastefulness, and that to the end of time there shall be creditors and debtors among men.

Meantime Shamadam was busy repairing his prestige as Senior. He called me once unto himself and in the privacy of his cell spoke to me as follows:

'You are the scribe and historian of this Ark; and you are a poor man's son. Your father has no land, yet has seven children and a wife to labour for and to provide with bare necessities. Record no word of this unfortunate episode lest those who shall come after us make of Shamadam stock for laughter. Desert this reprobate Mirdad, and I shall make your father a freeholder, and stock his granaries and fill his coffer full.'

To which I responded that God would care for my father and his family much better than Shamadam ever could. As to Mirdad I owned him as my master and deliverer, and sooner would desert my life than desert him. As to the records of the Ark, I shall keep them in good faith and to the best of my knowledge and ability.

I later learned that Shamadam had made similar proffers to everyone of the companions; but how successful they were I could not tell. It was noticeable, however, that Himbal was not so constant as before in his attendance of the Aerie.

# CHAPTER EIGHTEEN

## Mirdad divines the death of Himbal's Father and the circumstances thereof.
## He speaks of Death.
## Time is the greatest Juggler
## The Wheel of Time, its Rim and its Axis

*Naronda*: Much water had leapt down the mountains and swept into the sea when the Companions, lacking Himbal, were once more gathered round the Master in the Aerie.

The Master was discoursing on the Omniwill. But suddenly he stopped and said,

MIRDAD: Himbal is in distress and would come to us for relief, but his feet are too ashamed to carry him hither. Go and assist him, Abimar.

*Naronda*: Abimar went out and soon returned with Himbal who was shaking with sobs and had a most unhappy countenance.

MIRDAD: Come near me, Himbal.

Ah, Himbal, Himbal. Because your father died you let grief gnaw your heart and turn its blood to tears. What would you do when all your family die? What would you do when all the fathers and the mothers, and all the sisters and the brothers in this world pass out of and beyond the reach of your hands and eyes?

*Himbal*: Aye, Master. My father died a violent death. A steer he had recently bought gored his belly and crushed his skull but yestereve. I have just been told it by the messenger. Woe is me. Ah woe is me.

MIRDAD: And he died, it seems, at the very time when the fortunes of this world were about to smile to him.

*Himbal*: It is so, Master. It is even so.

MIRDAD: And his death pains you the keener because the steer was bought w⸱+h the money you had sent him.

*Himbal*: It is so, Master. It is even so. You seem to know all things.

MIRDAD: Which money was the price of your love for Mirdad.

*Naronda*: Himbal could speak no more; for he choked with tears.

MIRDAD: Your father is not dead, Himbal. Nor dead are yet his form and shadow. But dead, indeed, are your senses to your father's altered form and shadow. For there be forms so delicate, with shadow so attenuated that the coarse eye of man cannot detect.

The shadow of a cedar in the forest is not the same as the shadow of that cedar become a mast upon a ship, or a pillar in a temple, or a scaffolding for gallows. Nor is the shadow of that cedar in the sun the same as it is in the light of the moon, or the stars, or in the purple haze of dawn.

Yet that cedar, no matter how transformed, lives on as a cedar, though the cedars in the forest recognize it no longer as their sister of yore.

Can a silkworm on the leaf discern a sister in the worm pupating in the silk cocoon? Or can the latter see a sister in the silk-moth on the wing?

Can a grain of wheat in the earth know her kinship with a stalk of wheat above the earth?

Can the vapours in the air, or the waters in the sea, own as sisters and brothers the icicles in a mountain crevice?

Can the Earth discern a sister star in a meteor hurled unto her out of the deeps of Space?

Can the oak see itself in the acorn?

Because your father is now in a light to which your eye is not accustomed and in a form which you cannot discern, you say your father is no more. But Man's material self, no matter where transported and how changed, is bound to cast a shadow until dissolved entirely in the light of Man's God-Self.

A piece of wood, be it to-day a green branch on a tree and a peg in a wall to-morrow, continues to be wood and to change in form and shadow until consumed by the fire within it. Likewise shall Man continue to be man, when living as when dead, until the God in him consume him; which is to say, until he *understands* his oneness with The One. But that is not to be accomplished in that twinkling of an eye which men are pleased to designate as a lifetime.

All Time is lifetime, my Companions.

There are no halts and starts in Time. Nor are there caravanserais where travellers may stop for refreshments and rest.

Time is a continuity which overlaps itself. Its rear is coupled to its van. Nothing is ended and dismissed in Time; and nothing is begun and finished.

Time is a wheel created by the senses, and by the senses set a-whirling in the voids of Space.

You sense the bewildering change of seasons and you believe, therefore, that all is in the clutches of change. But you allow withal that the power which folds and unfolds the seasons is everlastingly one and the same.

You sense the growth of things and their decay, and you declare despondently that decay is the end of all growing things. But you avow that the force which makes for growth and decay itself neither grows nor decays.

You sense the speed of the wind in relation to the breeze; and you say that the wind is the swiftest by far. But despite that you admit that the mover of the wind and the mover of the breeze is one and the same and neither dashes with the wind, nor toddles with the breeze.

How credulous you are! How gullible of every trick your senses play on you! Where is your Imagination? For with it only can you see that all the changes which bewilder you are but a sleight of hand.

How can the wind be swifter than the breeze? Does not the breeze give birth to the wind? Does not the wind carry with it the breeze?

You, walkers on the Earth, how measure you the distances you walk with paces and with leagues? Whether you saunter or gallop, are you not carried on by the speed of the Earth into the spaces and regions whither the Earth herself is carried? Is not your gait, therefore, the same as the gait of the Earth? Is not the Earth, in turn, carried along by the other bodies, and her speed made equal to their speed?

Yea, the slow is the mother of the swift. The swift is the carrier of the slow. And the swift and slow are inseparable at every point of Time and Space.

How say you that growth is growth and decay is decay, and that the one is the other's enemy? Has anything ever sprung up except out of something decayed? Has anything ever decayed except from something growing?

Are you not growing by continually decaying? Are you not decaying by continually growing?

Are not the dead the subsoil of the living, and the living, the granaries of the dead?

If growth be the child of decay, and decay be the child of growth; if Life be the mother of Death, and Death be the mother of Life, then verily were they but one at every point of Time and Space. And verily were your joy for living and for growing so stupid as your grief for dying and decaying.

How say you that Autumn only is the season of grapes? I say that the grape is ripe in Winter, too, when it is but a drowsing sap pulsating imperceptibly and dreaming its dreams in the vine; and also in the Spring when it comes out in tender clusters of tiny beads of emerald; and also in the Summer when the clusters spread out and the beads swell up, and their cheeks become tinted with the gold of the Sun.

If every season carry in itself the other three, then verily were all the seasons one at every point of Time and Space.

Aye, Time is the greatest juggler, and men are the greatest dupes. Much like the squirrel in the wheel, Man who has set the wheel of Time a-turning is so enthralled and carried by the motion that he no longer can believe himself to be the mover, nor can he 'find the time' to stay the whir of Time.

And much like the cat that licks its tongue away in licking a whetstone believing the blood it licks to be seeping from the stone, Man licks his very blood spilled on the rim of Time, and munches his very flesh rent by the spokes of Time believing them to be the blood and flesh of Time.

The wheel of Time revolves in the voids of Space. Upon its rim are all the things perceivable by the senses which are unable to perceive a thing except in Time and Space. So things continue to appear and disappear. What disappears for one at a certain point of Time and Space appears to another at another point. What may be up to one is down to another. What may be day to one is to another night, depending on the 'When' and 'Where' of the looker on.

One is the road of Life and Death, O monks, upon the rim of the wheel of Time. For motion in a circle can never reach an end, nor ever spend itself. And every motion in the world is a motion in a circle.

Shall Man, then never free himself of the vicious circle of Time?

Man shall, because Man is heir to God's holy Freedom.

The wheel of time rotates, but its axis is ever at rest.

God is the axis of the wheel of Time. Though all things rotate about Him in Time and Space, yet is He always timeless and space-less and still. Though all things proceed from His Word, yet is His Word as timeless and spaceless as He.

In the axis all is peace. On the rim all is commotion. Where would you rather be?

I say to you, slip from the rim of Time into the axis and spare yourselves the nausea of motion. Let Time revolve about you; but you revolve not with Time.

## CHAPTER NINETEEN

## Logic and Faith
## Self-denial is Self-assertion
## How to arrest the Wheel of Time
## Weeping and Laughing

*Bennoon*: Forgive me, Master. But your logic confounds me with its illogicality.

MIRDAD: No wonder, Bennoon, you have been called 'the judge'. You would insist upon the *logic* of the case before you can decide it. Have you been judge so long and have not yet found out that the only use of Logic is to rid Man of Logic and lead him to Faith which leads to Understanding?

Logic is immaturity weaving its nets of gossamer wherewith it aims to catch the behemoth of knowledge. When Logic comes of age it strangles itself in its nets and then becomes transmuted into Faith, which is the deeper knowledge.

Logic is a crutch for the cripple; but a burden for the swift of foot; and a greater burden still for the winged.

Logic is Faith in dotage. Faith is Logic come of age. When your logic comes of age, Bennoon, as soon it shall, you would no longer speak of Logic.

*Bennoon*: To slip from the rim of Time into the axis we must perforce deny ourselves. Can man deny his own existence?

MIRDAD: For that, indeed, you must deny the self that is a plaything in the hands of Time and thus assert the Self which is immune to juggleries of Time.

*Bennoon*: Can the denial of one self be the assertion of another?

MIRDAD: Aye, to deny the self is to assert the Self. When one is dead to change, then one is born to changelessness. Most men live to die. Happy are they who die to live.

*Bennoon*: Yet dear is man's identity to man. How shall he sink in God and still be aware of his identity?

MIRDAD: Is it a loss for the brook to be lost in the Sea and thus be aware of itself as the Sea? For Man to lose his identity in God is but to lose his shadow and find the shadowless essence of his being.

*Micaster*: How can Man, a creature of Time, be free of the clutches of Time?

MIRDAD: As Death shall deliver you from Death, and Life shall release you from Life, so shall Time emancipate you from Time.

Man shall so weary of change that everything in him shall yearn, and yearn with unabating passion, for that which is mightier than change. And surely he shall find it in himself.

Happy are they that yearn, for they are already upon the threshold of Freedom. Them do I seek, and for them do I preach. Have I not chosen you because I heard your yearnings?

But woe to them who swing the rounds of Time and seek to find therein their freedom and their peace. No sooner do they smile for birth than they are made to weep for death. No sooner are they filled than they are emptied. No sooner do they trap the dove of peace than she is turned into a vulture of war in their hands. The more they think they know, the less in truth they know. The farther they advance, the farther they retreat. The higher they rise, the lower they fall.

For these my words shall be as vague and irritating murmurs; as prayers in a madhouse shall they be, and as torches lit before the blind. Not till they, too, begin to yearn for Freedom will they open their ears to my words.

*Himbal*: (Weeping) Not only my ears have you opened, Master, but also my heart. Forgive the deaf and blind Himbal of yesterday.

MIRDAD: Arrest your tears, Himbal. A tear does not become an eye that searches for horizons beyond the domains of Time and Space.

Let those who laugh when tickled by Time's cunning fingers weep when their skin is shredded by his nails.

Let those who dance and sing to radiance of Youth totter and moan to wrinkles of Old Age.

Let merrymakers at the carnivals of Time cover their heads with ashes at his funerals.

But you must ever be serene. In the kaleidoscope of change seek only the unchanging.

Nothing is worth a tear in Time. Nothing is worth a smile. A laughing face and a weeping face are equally unseemly and distorted.

Would you avoid the salt of tears? Avoid, then, the contortions of laughter.

A tear when volatilized becomes a giggle. A giggle when condensed becomes a tear.

Be neither volatile to joy, nor condensable to sorrow. But be serenely equable to both.

# CHAPTER TWENTY

# Where do We Go after We Die?
# On Repentance

*Micaster*: Master, where do we go after we die?

MIRDAD: Where are you now, Micaster?

*Micaster*: In the Aerie.

MIRDAD: Think you this Aerie large enough to contain you? Think you this Earth Man's only home?

Your bodies, though circumscribed in Time and Space, are drawn from everything in Time and Space. So much of you as comes from the Sun lives in the Sun. So much of you as comes from the Earth lives in the Earth. And so with all the other spheres and the trackless spaces between.

The foolish only like to think that Man's only abode is the Earth, and that the myriad bodies floating in the Space are but as ornaments for Man's abode and as distractions for his eyes.

The Morning Star, the Milky Way, the Pleiades are no less homes for Man than is this Earth. Each time they send a ray into his eye they lift him to themselves. Each time he passes under them he draws them to himself.

All things are incorporated into Man, and Man is in turn incorporated into them. The Universe is but a single body. Commune with the slightest particle thereof, and you commune with all.

And as you die continually when living, so do you live continally when dead; if not in this body, then in a body of another form. But you continue to live in a body until dissolved in God; which is to say, until you overcome all change.

*Micaster*: Do we return to this Earth as we journey from change to change?

MIRDAD: The law of Time is repetition. What once occurred in Time is bound to re-occur again and again; the intervals, in the case of Man, may be long or brief depending on the intensity of each man's desire and will for repetition.

When you pass out of the cycle known as life into the cycle known as death, and carry with you thirsts unquenched for the Earth and hungers unappeased for her passions, then will the magnet of the Earth draw you again to her bosom. And the Earth shall suckle you, and Time shall wean you life after life and death after death until you wean yourself, once and for all, of your own will and accord.

*Abimar*: Has our Earth power over you, too, Master? For you appear as one of us?

MIRDAD: I come when I will, and I go when I will, I come to free the tenants of the Earth from bondage to the Earth.

*Micayon*: I would be weaned away forever from the Earth. How can I do it, Master?

MIRDAD: By loving the Earth and all her children. When Love is the only residue of all your accounts with the Earth, then will the Earth acquit you of her debt.

*Micayon*: But Love is attachment, and attachment is bondage.

MIRDAD: Nay, Love is the only freedom from attachment. When you love everything, you are attached to nothing.

*Zamora*: Can one by Love escape the repetition of one's transgressions against Love and so arrest the wheel of Time?

MIRDAD: That you can attain by Repentance. A curse escaping your tongue will seek another lodging when it comes back and finds your tongue coated with loving benedictions. Thus Love will block the repetition of that curse.

A lustful glance will seek a lustful eye when it returns and finds the mother-eye brimming with loving glances. Thus Love will stay the repetition of that lustful glance.

A wicked wish launched by a wicked heart will seek a nest elsewhere when it returns and finds the mother-heart teeming with loving wishes. Thus Love will thwart the rebirth of that wicked wish.

That is Repentance.

Time can repeat for you nothing but Love when Love becomes your only residue. When one thing only is repeated at every place and time it then becomes a constancy filling all Time and Space and thus annihilating both.

*Himbal*: Yet one thing more troubles my heart and clouds my understanding. Master: Why did my father die this death and no other?

# CHAPTER TWENTY-ONE

# The Holy Omniwill
## Why things Happen as they do
## and When they do

MIRDAD: How strange that you, children of Time and Space, are not aware as yet that Time is the universal memory inscribed on the tablets of Space.

If you, being limited by the senses, can yet remember certain things between your birth and death, how much more so can Time which was before your birth and lasts indefinitely beyond your death?

I say to you that Time remembers everything at all – not only that of which you have a vivid recollection, but that as well of which you are entirely unaware.

For there is no oblivion in Time; no, not of the slightest movement, or breath, or whim. And all that is kept in the memory of Time is graven deep upon the things in Space.

The very earth you tread; the very air you breathe, the very houses you dwell in can readily reveal to you the most minute details in the records of your lives, past, present and to come, had you but the stamina to read and the keenness to grasp the meaning.

In life as in death; on the Earth as beyond the Earth, you never are alone, but are in constant company of things and beings which have their share in your life and death, as you have yours in their life and death. As you partake of them, so they partake of you; and as you seek them, so they seek you.

Man has a will in everything; and each thing has a will in Man. The interchange goes on uninterrupted. But a woefully bad accountant is the failing memory of Man. Not so the faultless memory of Time which keeps a most exact account of Man's relations with his fellow-men and all the other beings in the Universe, and forces him to settle his accounts each twinkling of an eye, life after life and death after death.

A thunderbolt would never strike a house except that house draw it to itself. The house is as much to account for its ruin as the bolt.

A bull would never gore a man except that man invite the bull to gore him. And verily that man is more to answer for his blood than is the bull.

The murdered whets the dagger of the murderer, and both deliver the fatal thrust.

The robbed directs the movements of the robber, and both commit the robbery.

Aye, Man invites his own calamities and then protests against the irksome guests, having forgotten how and when and where he penned and sent out the invitations. But Time does not forget; and Time delivers in due season each invitation to the right address; and Time conducts each invitee to the dwelling of the host.

I say to you, protest not any guest lest he avenge his slighted pride by tarrying too long, or by making his visits more frequent than otherwise he would consider meet.

Be kind and hospitable to all your guests whatever be their mien and their behaviour; for they in truth are but your creditors. Give the obnoxious ones in particular even more than is their due that they may go away thankful and satisfied, and should they visit you again, they would come back as friends and not as creditors.

Treat every guest as if he were the guest of honour, that you may gain his confidence and learn the hidden motives of his call.

Accept a misfortune as if it were a fortune. For a misfortune, once understood, is soon transformed into a fortune. While a fortune misconstrued quickly becomes a misfortune.

You choose your birth and death, their time and place and their manner as well despite your wayward memory which is a mesh of falsehoods with glaring holes and gaps.

The would-be wise declare that men have no part whatsoever in their birth and death. The indolent who squint at Time and Space through the narrow socket of the eye would readily dismiss most happenings in Time and Space as accidents. Beware of their conceit and deceit, my Companions.

There are no accidents in Time and Space. But all things are ordered by the Omniwill which neither errs in anything, nor overlooks a thing.

As drops of rain gather themselves in springs; and springs flow out to meet in brooks and rivulets; and rivulets and brooks offer themselves as tributaries to the larger streams; and mighty streams carry their waters to the seas; and seas assemble in the Greater Ocean, so does every will of every creature, inanimate or animate, flow as tributary into the Omniwill.

I say to you that everything has will. Even the stone, apparently so deaf, and dumb and lifeless, is not without a will. Else would it not have been, and would it not affect a thing, and nothing would affect it. Its consciousness of willing and of being may differ in degree from that of man, but not in substance.

How much of the life of a single day can you in truth assert you are conscious of? A very trifling part indeed.

If you, equipped with brains and memories and means of recording emotions and thoughts, are yet unconscious of the major part of a single day's living, why do you wonder that the stone is so unconscious of its life and will?

And as you live and move so much without being conscious of living and moving, so do you will as much without being conscious of willing. But the Omniwill is conscious of your unconsciousness and that of every creature in the Universe.

In redistributing itself, as is its wont at every moment of Time and every point of Space, the Omniwill gives back to every man and every thing whatever they had willed, no more, no less, whether they willed it consciously or otherwise. But men, not knowing that, are but too oft dismayed by what falls to their lot from the all-containing bag of The Omniwill. And men protest in dejection and blame their dismay upon the fickle Fate.

It is not Fate, O monks, that is fickle; for Fate is but another name of The Omniwill. It is Man's will that is as yet too fickle, and too fitful and too uncertain of its course. It dashes east to-day and west to-morrow. Here it stamps this thing as a good, and decries it there as an evil. Now it accepts this man as a friend, only to fight him later as an enemy.

Your will must not be fickle, my Companions. Know that all your relationships with things and men are determined by what you will of them, and they of you. And what you will of men and things determines what they will of you.

Therefore said I to you before, and say it now; Be careful how you breathe, and how you speak, and what you wish and think and do. For your will is hid even in every breath, and every word, and every wish and thought and deed. And what is hid from you is always manifest to The Omniwill.

Do not will of any man a pleasure that is to him a pain, lest your pleasure pain you more than pain.

Nor will of anything a good that is to it an evil, lest you be willing evil to yourselves.

But will of all men and all things their love; for with it only shall your veils be lifted, and Understanding dawn within your heart and thus initiate your will into the wondrous mysteries of The Omniwill.

Till you grow conscious of all things you cannot be conscious of their will in you, nor of your will in them.

Till you are conscious of your will in all things and of their will in you, you cannot know the mysteries of The Omniwill.

And till you know the mysteries of The Omniwill you must not set your will against it; for surely you shall be the loser. You shall come out of each encounter scarred and drunk with gall. And you shall seek revenge only to add new scars to the old and make the cup of gall overflow.

I say to you, accept The Omniwill if you would turn defeat to victory. Accept without a murmur all the things that fall to you from its mysterious bag; accept them in gratitude and in the faith that they are your just and due share in The Omniwill. Accept them with the will to understand their value and their meaning.

And once you understand the hidden ways of your own will, you understand The Omniwill.

Accept what you do not know that it may help you to know it. Resent it, and it shall remain an irritating puzzle.

Let your will be a maid to The Omniwill till Understanding make The Omniwill a servant to your will.

So taught I Noah.

So I teach you.

# CHAPTER TWENTY-TWO

## Mirdad relieves Zamora of his Secret
## And speaks of the Male and the Female
## of Marriage, of Celibacy
## and of the Overcomer

MIRDAD: Naronda, my faithful memory! What say to you these lilies?

*Naronda*: Nothing that I can hear, my Master.

MIRDAD: I hear them say, 'We love Naronda, and fain do we offer him our fragrant souls in token of our love.' Naronda, my constant heart! What say to you the waters in this pond?

*Naronda*: Nothing that I can hear, my Master.

MIRDAD: I hear them say, 'We love Naronda, therefore do we quench his thirst and the thirst of his beloved lilies.'

Naronda, my ever wakeful eye! What says to you this day with all the things it rocks so gently in its sun-lit arms?

*Naronda*: Nothing that I can hear, my Master.

MIRDAD: I hear it say, 'I love Naronda; therefore do I rock him so gently in my sun-lit arms together with the rest of my beloved family.'

With so much to love and to be loved by, is not Naronda's life too full for any idle dreams and thoughts to nest and hatch therein?

Verily, Man is the darling of the Universe. All things are glad to pamper him. But few are the men who are not spoiled by such a pampering, and fewer still the men who do not bite the hands that pamper them.

To the unspoiled even a snake bite is a loving kiss. But to the spoiled even a loving kiss is a snake bite. Is it not so, Zamora?

*Naronda*: So was the Master saying as he, Zamora and myself, of a sunny afternoon, were irrigating certain flower beds in the garden of the Ark. Zamora, who was all the while considerably distracted, low-spirited, and downcast, was brought to, as it were, and much taken aback by the Master's question.

*Zamora*: What the Master says is true the same must be true.

MIRDAD: Is it not true in your case, Zamora? Have you not been poisoned by many loving kisses? Are you not anguished now by the memory of your poisoned love?

*Zamora*: (Throwing himself at the Master's feet with tears gushing from his eyes) Oh, Master! How childish and vain of me, or any man, to hide a secret from your eye even in the inmost recesses of the heart!

MIRDAD: (As he raised Zamora to himself) How childish and vain to hide it even from these lilies!

*Zamora*: I know that my heart is not yet pure because my last night's dreams were impure.

This day I would purge my heart. I would strip it naked before you, my Master; before Naronda; before these lilies and the earthworms crawling among their roots. I would unburden my soul of my crushing secret. Let this languid breeze waft it to every creature in the world.

I loved a maiden in my youth. Fairer than the morning star was she. Her name to my tongue was sweeter by far than sleep to my eyelids. When you spoke to us on prayer and the bloodstream I was the first, I trow, to drink in the healing substance of your words. For Hoglah's love – that was the maiden's name – was the commander of my blood, and I knew what well-commanded blood could do.

With Hoglah's love eternity was mine. I wore it as a wedding ring. And Death himself I donned as a coat of mail. I felt me older than all yesterdays, and younger than the last to-morrow to be born. My arms supported the heavens, and my feet propelled the earth; while in my heart were many blazing suns.

But Hoglah died, and Zamora, the flaming phoenix, became a heap of ashes with no new phoenix to emerge out of the cold and lifeless heap. Zamora the fearless lion became a frightened hare. Zamora the pillar of the sky became a woeful wreck in a pool of stagnant waters.

I salvaged what I could of Zamora and made for this Ark hoping to bury myself alive in its diluvian memories and shadows. To my good fortune I arrived here just as a companion had departed this world, and I was taken in.

For fifteen years have the companions in this Ark seen and heard Zamora, but Zamora's secret they neither heard nor saw. Mayhap

the ancient walls and sombre passageways of the Ark are not unaware of it. Mayhap the trees, the flowers and the birds in this
garden know somewhat of it. But surely the strings of my harp can
tell you more, O Master, of my Hoglah than I can.

Just as your words began to warm and stir Zamora's ashes, and I
was nigh assured of new Zamora's birth, Hoglah visits my dreams
and sets my blood a-boiling, and tosses me unto the sullen crags of
this day's reality a burnt out torch, a stillborn ecstasy, a heap of
lifeless ashes.

Ah Hoglah, Hoglah!

Forgive me, Master. I cannot restrain my tears. Shall flesh be
aught but flesh? Pity my flesh. Pity Zamora.

MIRDAD: Pity itself is in need of pity. Mirdad has none of it. But
love abundant has Mirdad for all things, even for the flesh; and more
so for the Spirit that takes the grosser form of flesh only to melt it in
its own formlessness. And Mirdad's love shall raise Zamora from
his ashes and make of him an overcomer.

The Overcomer do I preach – Man unified and master of himself.

Man made a prisoner by the love of woman, and woman made a
prisoner by the love of man are equally unfit for Freedom's precious
crown. But man and woman made as one by Love, inseparable,
indistinguishable, are verily entitled to the prize.

No love is Love that subjugates the Lover.

No love is Love that feeds on flesh and blood.

No love is Love that draws a woman to a man only to breed more
women and more men and thus perpetuate their bondage to the flesh.

The Overcomer do I preach – The Phoenix-Man who is too free
to be a male, too sublimated to be a female.

As in the denser spheres of Life the male and the female are one,
so are they one in Life's rarer spheres. The interval between is but
a segment in eternity dominated by the illusion of Duality. Those
who can see neither before nor aft believe this segment of eternity
to be itself Eternity. They cling to the delusion of Duality as if it
were of Life its very core and essence, not knowing that the rule of
Life is Unity.

A stage in Time is Duality. As it proceeds from Unity, so does it
lead to Unity. The quicker you traverse this stage the sooner you
embrace your freedom.

And what are man and woman but the single Man unconscious of his singleness and so cloven in twain and made to quaff the gall of Duality that he may yearn for the nectar of Unity; and yearning, seek it with a will; and seeking, find it and possess it, conscious of its surpassing liberty?

Let the stallion whinny to the mare, and the doe call to the buck. Nature herself urges them on and blesses and applauds their act, for they are conscious of no higher destiny as yet than that of self-reproduction.

Let men and women who are yet not far from the stallion and the mare, and from the buck and the doe, seek each the other in the dark seclusions of the flesh. Let them alloy the licentiousness of the bed chamber with the licence of wedlock. Let them take joy in the fertility of their backs and the fecundity of their wombs. Let them propagate the species. Nature herself is glad to be their sponsor and midwife; and Nature spreads them couches of roses forgetting not the pricks.

But men and women yearners must realize their unity even while in the flesh; not by communion of the flesh, but by the Will to Freedom from the flesh and all the impediments it places in their way to perfect Unity and Holy Understanding.

You often hear men speak of 'human nature' as if it were a rigid element, well measured, well defined, exhaustively explored and firmly bounded on all sides by something they call *Sex*.

To gratify sex passions is human nature. But to harness their turbulent onrush and use it as a means for overcoming sex is to go decidedly against human nature, and suffer in the end. So they say. Lend not an ear to their prattle.

Too vast is Man and too imponderable his nature. Too varied are his talents, and too inexhaustible his strength. Beware of those who attempt to set him boundaries.

The flesh, to be sure, levies on Man a heavy tribute. But he pays it only for a time. Who of you would be a vassal all eternity? Which vassal does not dream of throwing off the yoke of his prince and then relieve himself of tribute paying?

Man was not born to be a vassal, not even to his manhood. And Man is ever yearning for freedom from vassalage of every kind. And Freedom shall surely be his.

What is a blood relationship to one who wills to overcome? A tie which must be broken with a will.

The Overcomer feels his blood related to all blood. Therefore is he tied to none.

Let the non-yearners reproduce the race. The yearners have another race to propagate – even the race of overcomers.

The race of overcomers descends not from back and womb. Rather does it ascend from celibate hearts whose blood is commanded by a dauntless will to overcome.

I know that you and many more like you throughout the world have taken vows of celibacy. Yet are you far from being celibate, as witnesses Zamora's last night's dream.

Not celibate are they who wear monastic garb and shut themselves away behind thick walls and massive iron gates. Many a monk and nun are lewder than the lewdest, though their flesh swear – and very truthfully – that it never communed with any other flesh. But celibate are they whose hearts and minds are celibate, whether they be in cloisters, or in the public marts.

Revere, my Companions, the Woman and sanctify her. Not as the mother of the race, nor as a consort or a lover, but as the twin of man and as his partner, share for share, in the long toil and suffering of dual life. For without her man cannot traverse the segment of Duality. But in her shall he find his unity, and in him shall she find her freedom from Duality. And the twins shall in time be joined in one – even the Overcomer who is nor male nor female; who is the Perfect Man.

The Overcomer do I preach – Man unified and master of himself. And each of you shall be an overcomer ere Mirdad lifts himself from your midst.

*Zamora*: It saddens my heart to hear you speak of leaving us. Should the day ever come when we shall seek you and find you not, Zamora will surely put an end to his breath.

MIRDAD: You can will many things, Zamora – you can will all things. But one thing can you not will, and that is to put an end to your will, which is the will of Life, which is the Omniwill. For Life which is Being can never will its own non-being; nor can non-being have a will. Nay, not even God can end Zamora.

As to my leaving you, the day shall surely come when you shall seek me in the flesh and not find me. For I have work to do elsewhere than on this Earth. But nowhere do I leave my work undone. Be of good cheer, therefore. Mirdad shall not part with you before he has made you overcomers – men unified and perfectly self-mastered.

When you shall have gained self-mastery and Unity, then shall you find Mirdad a constant dweller in your hearts, and his name shall never tarnish in your memory.

So taught I Noah.

So I teach you.

# CHAPTER TWENTY-THREE

# Mirdad heals Sim-Sim
## and Speaks on Old Age

*Naronda*: Sim-Sim, the oldest cow in the stables of the Ark, had been ailing for five days and would not touch any feed or water, when Shamadam sent for a butcher saying that it was more prudent to slaughter the cow and profit by the sale of her meat and hide than let her die and be a total loss.

When the Master heard of it he became exceeding thoughtful and straightway hurried to the stable and into Sim-Sim's stall. The Seven followed in his wake.

Sim-Sim stood sad and almost motionless, her head hanging low, her eyes half-shut and her hair bristling and devoid of sheen. Now and then would she barely move an ear to chase away an impertinent fly. Her great milk-bag hung limp and empty between her thighs; for Sim-Sim towards the end of her long and fruitful life was denied the sweet heartaches of motherhood. Her hip-bones jutted out, grim and forlorn, like two tombstones. Her ribs and vertebrae could easily be counted. Her long and slender tail, with a heavy tuft of hair at the end, fell straight and stiff.

The Master approached the ailing animal and began to stroke her between the horns and eyes and under the chin. Occasionally he would pass his hand over her back and belly, speaking to her all the while as he would speak to a human being:

MIRDAD: Where is your cud, my generous Sim-Sim? So much has Sim-Sim given that she forgot to leave herself even a small cud to chew. And much has Sim-Sim yet to give. Her snow-white milk is till this day running crimson in our veins. Her sturdy calves are trailing heavy ploughs in our fields and helping us to feed many a hungry mouth. Her graceful heifers fill our pastures with their young. Even her refuse graces our board in succulent greens from the garden and luscious fruits from the orchard.

Our ravines still echo and re-echo good Sim-Sim's lungful bellowing. Our springs still mirror her benign and lovely face. Our soil still cherishes and guards with jealousy the ineffaceable prints of her hoofs.

Too glad are our grasses to feed Sim-Sim. Too pleased is our sun to caress her. Too happy are our breezes to glide over her soft and glossy fur. Too thankful is Mirdad to see her through the desert of Old Age and be her guide to other pastures in the land of other suns and breezes.

Much has Sim-Sim given, and much has she taken; but more has Sim-Sim yet to give and to take.

*Micaster*: Can Sim-Sim understand your words that you should speak to her as if she had a human understanding?

MIRDAD: It is not the word that counts, good Micaster. It is what vibrates in the word. And to that even a beast is susceptible. Besides, I see a woman looking at me out of meek Sim-Sim's eye.

*Micaster*: What is the good of speaking so to aged and failing Sim-Sim? Hope you thereby to stay the ravages of age and lengthen Sim-Sim's days?

MIRDAD: A dreadful burden is Old Age to man as well as to beast. And men have made it doubly so by their neglectful heartlessness. Upon a new born babe they lavish their utmost care and affection. But to an age-burdened man they reserve their indifference more than their care, and their disgust more than their sympathy. Just as impatient as they are to see a suckling grow into manhood, just so impatient are they to see an old man swallowed by the grave.

The very young and the very old are equally helpless. But the helplessness of the young conscripts the loving, sacrificial help of all. While the helplessness of the old is able to command but the grudging help of few. Verily, the old are more deserving of sympathy than the young.

When the word must knock long and loud to gain admittance to an ear once sensitive and alert to the faintest whisper,

When the once limpid eye becomes a dancing floor for the weirdest blotches and shadows,

When the once winged foot becomes a lump of lead, and the hand that moulded life becomes a broken mould,

When the knee is out of joint, and the head is a puppet on the neck,

When the mill-stones are ground out, and the mill itself is a dreary cave,

When to rise is to sweat with the fear of falling down, and to sit is to sit with the painful doubt of never rising again,

When to eat and drink is to dread the aftermath of eating and drinking, and not to eat and drink is to be stalked by hateful Death,

Aye, when Old Age is upon a man, then is the time, my companions, to lend him ears and eyes, and give him hands and feet, and brace his failing strength with love so as to make him feel that he is no whit less dear to Life in his waning years than he was in his waxing babyhood and youth.

Four-score years may not be more than a wink in eternity. But a man who has sown himself for four-score years is much more than a wink. He is the foodstuff for all who harvest his life. And which life is not harvested by all?

Are you not harvesting even this very moment the life of every man and woman that ever walked this Earth? What is your speech but the harvest of their speech? What are your thoughts but the gleanings of their thoughts? Your very clothes and dwellings, your food, your implements, your laws, your traditions and conventions, are they not the clothes, the dwellings, the food, the implements, the laws, the traditions and conventions of those who had been and gone before?

Not one thing do you harvest at one time, but all things and at all times. You are the sowers, the harvest, the reapers, the field and the threshing-floor. If your harvest be poor, look to the seed you have sown in others and the seed you allowed them to sow in you. Look also to the reaper and his sickle, and to the field and the threshing-floor.

An old man whose life you have harvested and put away in granaries is surely worthy of your utmost care. Should you embitter with indifference his years which are yet rich with things to be harvested, that which you have gathered of him and put away, and that which you are yet to gather would certainly be bitter in your mouth. So is it with a failing beast.

It is not right to profit by the crop, and then to curse the sower and the field.

Be kind to men of every race and clime, my companions. They

are the food for your God-ward journey. But be especially kind to men in their old age lest through unkindness your food be spoiled and you never reach your journey's end.

Be kind to animals of every sort and age. They are your dumb but very faithful helpers in the long and arduous preparations for the journey. But be especially kind to animals in their old age, lest through the hardness of your heart their faithfulness be turned into faithlessness, and their help become an hindrance.

It is a rank ingratitude to thrive on Sim-Sim's milk, and when she has no more to give, to lay the butcher's knife to her throat.

*Naronda*: Hardly had the Master finished saying that when Shamadam with the butcher walked in. The butcher went straight to Sim-Sim. No sooner did he see her than we heard him shout in joyful mockery, 'How say you this cow is ill and dying? She is healthier than I, excepting that she is starved – the poor animal – and I am not. Give her to eat.'

And great was our amazement, indeed, when we looked at Sim-Sim and saw her chewing the cud. Even Shamadam's heart softened, and he ordered the best of cow-delicacies brought to Sim-Sim. And Sim-Sim ate with a relish.

# CHAPTER TWENTY-FOUR

# Is it Lawful to Kill to Eat?

WHEN Shamadam and the butcher had departed Micayon asked the Master, saying:

*Micayon*: Is it not lawful, Master, to kill to eat?

MIRDAD: To feed on Death is to become food for Death. To live by others' pain is to become a prey for pain. So has decreed the Omniwill. Know that and choose your course, Micayon.

*Micayon*: If I had my choice, I would choose to live, like a phoenix, on the aroma of things, not on their flesh.

MIRDAD: An excellent choice, indeed. Believe, Micayon, that the day is coming in which men shall live by the aroma of things, which is their spirit, and not by their flesh and blood. And that day is not far off for the yearners.

For the yearners know that the life of flesh is but the bridge to the fleshless Life.

And the yearners know that the coarse and inadequate senses are but the peepholes into the world of the infinitely fine and adequate sense.

And the yearners know that every flesh they tear they must inevitably repair, soon or late, with their own flesh; and every bone they crush they must rebuild with their own bone; and every drop of blood they spill they must replenish with their own blood. For that is the law of flesh.

And the yearners would be free of bondage to this law. Therefore do they reduce their bodily wants to the lowest minimum, reducing thereby their debt to the flesh which is, in truth, a debt to Pain and Death.

The yearner is inhibited by his own will and yearning; while the non-yearner waits on others to prohibit him. A multitude of things which are, to the non-yearner, lawful, the yearner makes unlawful for himself.

While the non-yearner grasps for more and yet more things to put away in his pocket or belly, the yearner walks his way without a pocket, and with a belly clean of any creature's blood and convulsions.

What the non-yearner gains – or thinks he gains – in bulk the yearner gains in lightness of spirit and sweetness of understanding.

Of two men looking at a green field one estimates its yield in bushels and calculates the price of the bushels in silver and in gold. The other drinks the greenness of the field with his eye, and kisses every blade with his thought, and fraternizes in his soul with every rootlet and pebble, and every clod of earth.

I say to you, the latter is the rightful owner of that field, although the other own it in fee simple.

Of two men sitting in a house one is the owner, the other, but a guest. The owner expatiates on the cost of building and main-tenance, and on the values of draperies and tapestries and other trappings and furnishings. While the guest blesses in his heart the hands that quarried, dressed and built the stone; and the hands that wove the tapestries and the draperies; and the hands that invaded the forest and turned it into windows and doors and into chairs and tables. And he is exalted in spirit in exalting the Creative Hand that caused these things to be.

I say to you, the guest is the permanent dweller in that house; while the nominal owner is but a beast of burden carrying the house on his back but dwelling not therein.

Of two men sharing with a calf the milk of that calf's mother one eyes the calf with the thought that his tender flesh would provide good meat for him and his friends to feast upon at his approaching birthday. The other thinks of the calf as his brother of the teat and is filled with affection for the young beast and his mother.

I say to you, the latter is truly nourished by that calf's meat; while the first is poisoned thereby.

Aye, many things are put in the belly that should be put in the heart.

Many things are shut in the pocket and the larder that should be shut in the eye and the nose.

Many things are crushed with the teeth that should be crushed with the mind.

Very little does the body need to sustain it. The less you give it, the more it gives you in return. The more you give it, the less it gives you in return.

Verily, things outside your larder and belly sustain you more than when in the larder and the belly.

But since you are unable yet to live by the fragrance alone of things, take unafraid your need – but no more than your need – of the generous heart of the Earth. For the Earth is so hospitable and loving that her heart is ever spread before her children.

How else can the Earth be, and where could she go outside of herself to feed herself? The Earth must feed the Earth, and the Earth is not a miserly hostess, but her board is ever spread and full for all.

In the same manner as the Earth invites you to her board, withholding nothing from your reach, in that same manner must you invite the Earth to your board and say to her in utmost love and sincerity:

'O mother inexpressible! As you have laid your heart before me to take of it my need, so do I lay my heart before you to take of it your need.'

If that be your guiding spirit in eating of the heart of the Earth, then little does it matter what you eat.

But if that be, indeed, your guiding spirit, then should you have the wisdom and the love not to bereave the Earth of any of her children, especially those which have come to feel the pleasure of living and the pain of dying – those that have arrived at the segment of Duality. For they, too, have their road to wend, slowly and laboriously, towards Unity. And their road is longer than yours. Delay them in their march, and they shall delay you in your march.

*Abimar*: Since all living things are doomed to die, through one cause or another, why should I have any scruples if I be the cause of any animal's death?

MIRDAD: While it is true that all the living are condemned to die, yet woe to him who is the cause of death of any living thing.

As you would not commission me to kill Naronda, knowing that I love him much and that no blood lust is in my heart, likewise the Omniwill would commission no man to kill a fellowman, or an animal, except it find him fit as an instrument for killing.

So long as men are what they are, so long shall there be thefts and robberies among them, and lies and wars and murders and every kind of dark and evil passions.

But woe to the thief and the robber; and woe to the liar and the war lord, and to the murderer and every man who harbours dark and evil passions in his heart. For they, being full of woe, are used by the Omniwill as messengers of woe.

But you, my Companions, must cleanse your hearts of every dark and evil passion that the Omniwill may find you fit to carry to the suffering world the joyful message of relief from suffering; the message of overcoming; the message of Freedom through Love and Understanding.

So taught I Noah.

So I teach you.

# CHAPTER TWENTY-FIVE

# Day of the Vine and the Preparation therefor
# Mirdad found Missing on the Eve thereof

*Naronda*: The Day of the Vine was drawing nigh, and we of the Ark, including the Master, together with squadrons of volunteer helpers from the outside, were busy night and day making ready for the great feast. The Master worked with so much zeal and was so unsparing of his strength that even Shamadam commented on the fact with evident satisfaction.

The vast cellars of the Ark had to be swept and white-washed, and scores of great wine-jars and barrels cleaned and arranged to receive the new wine; while as many jars and barrels containing wine of last year's vintage had to be properly displayed for buyers to taste and to examine their contents. For the custom is to sell on each Vine Day the wine of the year preceding.

The spacious courts of the Ark were to be tidied and groomed well and hundreds of tents and booths were to be pitched and built therein for pilgrims to live and traders to display their wares for the whole week's duration of festivities.

The great winepress had to be put in order and made ready to receive untold quantities of grapes which were to be brought to the Ark by its many tenants and patrons on donkey, mule and camel back. Enormous quantities of bread had to be baked and other provisions prepared to be sold to those who run short of provisions or who come entirely provisionless.

Originally an occasion for thanksgiving the Day of the Vine, thanks to Shamadam's unusual business sense and acumen, has been stretched unto a week and turned into a sort of fair to which men and women of all walks of life, from near and far, flocked in annually growing numbers. Princes and paupers, soil tillers and artisans, profit seekers, pleasure seekers and seekers of other ends; drunkards and total abstainers; pious pilgrims and impious tramps; men of the temple and men of the tavern, with herds of beasts of burden – such is the motley horde that invades the quiet of Altar

Peak twice every year, on the Day of the Vine in the Fall and the Day of the Ark in the Spring.

No pilgrim comes to the Ark on either of these occasions with empty hands; but all bring gifts of one kind or another, the gifts varying from a cluster of grapes or a pine cone to a string of pearls or a diamond necklace. While a tax of ten per-centum of their sales is levied on all the traders.

It is the custom on the opening day of festivities for the Senior, seated on a high platform beneath a great arbour hung with bunches of grapes, to welcome and bless the crowd, then to bless and receive their gifts, and then to drink with them the first cup of the new vintage. He would pour himself a cup out of a great longneck, hollowed gourd, then hand that gourd over to one of the Companions to be passed round to the multitudes, refilling it each time it was emptied. And when all had filled their cups the Senior would ask them to raise them high and sing with him the Hymn to the Sacred Vine which is said to have been sung by father Noah and his family when they first tasted of the blood of the Vine. And having sung the hymn, the crowd would empty their cups with shouts of joy and then disperse to pursue their various trades and pleasures.

And this is the Hymn to the Sacred Vine:

> Hail the Sacred Vine!
>
> Hail the wondrous root
> That feeds her tender shoot
> And fills her golden fruit
> With vivifying wine.
> Hail the Sacred Vine!
>
> Orphans of the Flood,
> Stranded in the mud,
> Taste and bless the blood
> Of the branch benign.
> Hail the Sacred Vine!
>
> You, hostages of clay,
> You, pilgrims gone astray,
> The Ransom and the Way

## Day of the Vine

Are in the plant divine –
The Vine, The Vine, The Vine!

On the morning of the day before the opening of festivities the Master was found missing. The Seven were alarmed beyond words, and they immediately instituted a most thorough search. All day and all night, with torches and lanterns did they seek, in the Ark and the vicinity; but no trace could they find of the Master. Shama-dam showed so much concern and appeared to be so perturbed that no one suspected his hand in the mysterious disappearance. Yet all were convinced that the Master had fallen victim of some foul play.

The great festivities were on, but the Seven were stricken dumb with sadness and moved about like shadows. The crowd had sung the hymn and drunk the wine, and the Senior had descended from the high platform when a voice was heard shouting high above the din and clatter of the crowd, 'We want to see Mirdad. We want to hear Mirdad.'

The voice we recognized as that of Rustidion who had spread far and wide all that the Master had said and done unto him. Quickly his shouting was taken up by the multitude, and the clamour for the Master became general and deafening which brimmed our eyes with tears and clamped our throats as with a vice.

Suddenly the tumult subsided, and a great hush fell on the crowd. And scarce could we believe our eyes when we looked and saw the Master on the high platform waving his hand for silence.

# CHAPTER TWENTY-SIX

## Mirdad Harangues the Pilgrims
## to the Day of the Vine
## and Relieves the Ark of some Dead Weight

MIRDAD: Behold Mirdad, the vine whose crop is still unharvested, whose blood is yet undrunk.

Heavy is Mirdad with his crop. But the harvesters, alas, are busy in other vineyards.

And choking is Mirdad with an overflow of blood. But the cup-bearers and the drinkers are fast adrunk with other wines.

Men of the plough and pick and pruning-hook, I bless your ploughs and picks and pruning-hooks.

What have you ploughed and picked and pruned until this day?

Have you ploughed up the dreary wastelands in your souls, so overgrown with all manner of weed, and thus become a veritable jungle where fearsome beasts and hideous reptiles thrive and multiply?

Have you picked out the noxious roots entwining in the dark and strangling your roots, and thus nipping your fruitage in the bud?

Or have you pruned away those branches of yourselves which are hollowed by busy worms, or withered by onslaughts of parasites?

Well have you learnt to plough and pick and prune your vineyards of the earth. But the unearthly vineyard which is you lies woefully waste and unhusbanded.

How very vain are all your labours except you attend to the vineyardist before the vineyard!

Men of the calloused hand! I bless your callouses.

Friends of the plumbline and rule; companions of the hammer and the anvil; road-fellows of the chisel and the saw, how skilled and competent you are in all your chosen crafts!

You know how to find of things their level and their depth. But your own depth and level you know not how to find.

Deftly do you shape a raw piece of iron with the hammer and the anvil. But the raw man you know not how to shape with the hammer of Will on the anvil of Understanding. Nor have you learnt of the anvil the priceless lesson of how to be struck without the slightest thought of striking back.

And clever are you with the chisel and the saw in wood and rock alike. But man uncouth and gnarled you know not how to render gainly and smooth.

How very vain are all your crafts except you first apply them to the craftsman!

Men trafficking for gain in the needs of men for the bounties of their Mother-Earth and the products of the hands of their fellow-men!

I bless the needs, the bounties and the products, and bless the traffic, too. But the gain itself, which is in truth a loss, finds not a blessing in my mouth.

When in the fateful hush of night you strike the balance of the day's proceeds, what do you set to profit, what, to loss? Set you to profit moneys realized above and over cost? Then worthless, indeed, were the day which you had traded away for a sum of money no matter how great. And lost to you were all its infinite riches of harmony, peace and light. Lost also its incessant calls to Freedom; and lost the hearts of men it held for you as gifts upon its palm.

When your main concern is with the pocketbooks of men, how can you find your way into their hearts? And save you find your way into men's hearts, how can you hope to reach the heart of God? And save you reach the heart of God, what life have you?

If that which you esteem a profit be a loss, how very great must be the loss!

Vain, indeed, is all your trading except the profits be accounted Love and Understanding.

Men of the sceptre and the crown!

A serpent is the sceptre in the hand that is too quick to wound but too slow to apply the healing ointments. While in the hand dispensing balm of Love the sceptre is a lightning-rod forestalling gloom and doom.

Examine well your hands.

A crown of gold, studded with diamond, ruby and sapphire, sits very cumbrous, sad and ill at ease upon the head swollen with vainglory, ignorance and lust for power over men. Aye, such a crown, so pedestalled, is but a stinging mockery of its own pedestal. Whereas a crown of the rarest and most exquisite gems would be too bashful of its own unworth to sit upon a head haloed with Understanding and victory over self.

Examine well your heads.

Would you be rulers of men? Learn first to rule yourselves.

How else can you rule well except you be well self-ruled? Can a wind-whipped, foaming wave give peace and quiet to the Sea? Can a tearful eye project a blissful smile into a tearful heart? Can a fear- or anger-shaken hand keep a ship on an even keel?

The rulers of men are ruled by men. And men are full of tumult, anarchy and chaos. For like the sea they lie exposed to every wind of heaven. And like the sea they ebb and flow and seem at times as if about to override the shore. But like the sea their depths are calm and immune to the lashes of winds on the surface.

If you would truly govern men, dive to their utmost depths. For men are more than foaming waves. But to dive to the utmost depths of men you must first dive to your own utmost depth. And to accomplish that you must lay down the sceptre and the crown that the hand may be free to feel, and the head unencumbered to think and to estimate.

Vain is all your rule, and lawlessness are all your laws, and chaos is all your order except you learn to rule the intractable man in you whose favourite hobby is to play with sceptres and with crowns.

Men of the censer and the Book! What burn you in the censer? What read you in the Book?

Burn you the amber blood that oozes and congeals out of the fragrant hearts of certain plants? But that is bought and sold in the public marts, and a penny's worth thereof can fully discommode any god.

Think you the smell of incense can drown out the stench of hatred, envy, greed? Of quibbling eyes, prevaricating tongues, lascivious hands? Of unbelief parading as belief, and sordid earth-liness blowing the horn of blissful paradise?

More pleasant in the nostrils of your God would be the smell of all these things starved unto death and one by one cremated in the heart, and their ashes scattered to the four Winds of heaven.

What burn you in the censer? Propitiation, praise and supplica-tion?

A wrathful god is better left to burst with his wrath. A praise-hungry god is better left to starve for praise. A hard-hearted god is better left to die of the hardness of his heart.

But neither wrathful, praise-hungry, nor hard of heart is God. Rather are you full of wrath, and hungry for praise and hard of heart.

Not incense would God have you burn, but your wrath and pride and heartlessness that you may be like Him free and omnipotent. And he would have your hearts be the censers.

What read you in the Book?

Read you commandments to be writ in gold upon the walls and domes of temples? Or living truths to be engraved upon the heart?

Read you doctrines to be taught from pulpits and zealously defended with logic, trickeries of speech, and if need be, with money and the edge of the sword? Or read you Life which is not a doctrine to be taught and defended, but a Way to be walked with a will to Freedom, in the temple as outside of it, in the night as in the day, and in the low places as in the high? And except you walk that Way and be certain of its goal, how can you have the temerity to invite the others to walk it?

Or read you charts, and maps, and price-lists in the Book showing men how much of heaven can be bought with so or so much of the earth?

Tricksters and agents of Sodom! You would sell Heaven unto men and take their share of the Earth as the price. You would make a gehenna of the Earth and urge men to flee it while you entrench yourselves the deeper therein. Why do you not make men sell their share in Heaven for a share in the Earth?

Did you read well your Book, you would show men how to make an heaven of the Earth. For to the heavenly-hearted the Earth is an heaven. While to the earthly-hearted the Heaven is an earth.

Uncover Heaven in the hearts of men by levelling therein all bars between Man and his fellow-men; between Man and all the creatures; between Man and God. But for that you must be heavenly-hearted yourselves.

Not a garden in bloom is Heaven to be bought or rented. But a state of being is Heaven attainable as well upon the Earth as anywhere within this boundless Universe. Why crane your necks and strain your eyes beyond?

Nor a raging furnace is Hell to be escaped with much praying and incense burning. But a state of the heart is Hell experienced as well on the Earth as anywhere in this uncharted immensity.

Where would you flee the fire whose fuel is the heart unless you flee the heart?

Vain is the search for Heaven, and vain the evasion of Hell so long as Man is held by his shadow. For both Heaven and Hell are states inherent in Duality. Except Man become single of mind, single of heart and single of body; except he be shadowless and single of Will, he shall always have one foot in Heaven and another in Hell. And that is Hell indeed.

Aye, it is more than Hell to have wings of light and feet of lead; to be buoyed up by hope and dragged down by despair; to be unfurled by fearless faith and furled by fearful doubt.

No heaven is heaven which is to others hell. No hell is hell which is to others heaven. And since one's hell is oft another's heaven, and one's heaven is oft another's hell, then Heaven and Hell were not enduring and conflicting states, but stages to be passed on the long pilgrimage to Freedom from both.

Pilgrims of the Sacred Vine!

No heavens has Mirdad to sell or grant to those who would be righteous. No hells to hold as scarecrows to the ones who would be wicked.

Except your righteousness be its own heaven it shall bloom for a day and then wither away.

Except your wickedness be its own scarecrow it shall sleep for a day and come to bloom at the first favourable season.

No hells and heavens has Mirdad to offer you, but Holy Understanding which lifts you far beyond the fire of any hell and the luxuriance of any heaven. Not with the hand, but with the heart must you receive this gift. For that the heart must needs be disencumbered of every stray desire and will save the desire and will to understand.

No strangers are you to the Earth; nor is the Earth to you a stepmother. But a very heart of her very heart are you, and a very backbone of her very backbone. Glad is she to bear you on her sturdy, broad and steady back. Why do you insist on bearing her upon your puny, fallen chests and moan, and puff and gasp for breath in consequence?

Flowing with milk and honey are the udders of the Earth. Why do you let both sour with your greed by taking of them more than you need?

Serene and comely is the face of the Earth. Why would you mar and ruffle it with bitter strife and fear?

A perfect unit is the Earth. Why do you persist in dismembering her with swords and boundary-marks?

Obedient and carefree is the Earth. Why are you so full of care and insubordination?

Yet more enduring are you than the Earth, than the Sun and all the spheres in the heavens. All shall pass away, but you shall not. Why tremble you as leaves in the wind?

If nothing else can make you feel your oneness with the Universe, the Earth alone should make you feel it. Yet Earth herself is but the mirror wherein your shadows are reflected. Is the mirror more than the mirrored? Is the shadow cast by a man more than the man?

Rub your eyes and be awake. For you are more than earth. Your destiny is more than to live and die and to provide abundant food for the ever-hungry jaws of Death. Your destiny is to be free from living and from dying; from Heaven and Hell and all the warring opposites incumbent on Duality. Your destiny is to be fruitful vines in the eternally fruitful vineyard of God.

As a living branch of a living vine, when buried in the ground, strikes root and ultimately becomes an independent, grape-bearing vine like its mother with which it remains connected, so shall Man, the living branch of the Vine Divine, when buried in the soil of his divinity, become a god, remaining permanently one with God.

Shall Man be buried alive that he may come to Life?

Yea and yea again. Except you be buried to duality of life and death you shall not rise to singleness of Being.

Except you be fed with the grapes of Love you shall not be filled with the wine of Understanding.

And except you be drunk with the wine of Understanding you shall not be sobered by the kiss of Freedom.

Not Love do you eat when you eat of the fruit of the earthly vine. You eat a greater hunger in order to appease a lesser one.

Not Understanding do you drink when you drink the blood of the earthly vine. You drink but a brief forgetfulness of pain the which, when spent, doubles the keenness of your pain. You flee from an irksome self only to meet that self around the corner.

The grapes that Mirdad offers you are not exposed to mould and rot. To be once filled with them is to remain forever full. The wine he has distilled for you is too strong for the lips afraid of being burnt, but quickening to the hearts that would be drunk with self-forgetfulness unto eternity.

Are there among you men enhungered for my grapes? Let them come forward with their baskets.

Are there any athirst for my blood? Let them bring their cups.

For heavy is Mirdad with his crop, and choking with an overflow of blood.

A day of self-forgetfulness was the Day of the Sacred Vine. A day intoxicated with the wine of Love and bathed in the glow of Understanding. A day ecstatic with the rhythmic beat of Freedom's wings. A day of levelling bars and merging one in all and all in one. But, lo! What has it become to-day?

It has become a week of morbid self-assertion; of sordid greed trading in sordid greed; of slavery frolicking with slavery, and ignorance debauching ignorance.

The Ark herself, once a distillery of Faith, and Love and Freedom has now been turned into a huge wine-press and monstrous trading mart. She takes the yield of your vineyards and sells it back to you as stupifying wine. The labour of your hands she forges into fetters for your hands. The sweat of your brows she turns into live embers wherewith to brand your brows.

Far, too far, has the Ark swerved from her chartered course. But now her rudder is set right. She would be rid of all dead weight that she may ply her course with ease and safety.

Therefore shall all gifts be returned to the givers, and all debts be remitted to the debtors. The Ark knows no giver but God, and God would have no man in debt, not even to Himself.

So taught I Noah.

So I teach you.

# CHAPTER TWENTY-SEVEN

## Should Truth be preached to All
## or to the Chosen Few?
## Mirdad reveals the Secret of his Disappearance
## on the Eve of the Day of the Vine
## and Speaks on Counterfeit Authority

*Naronda*: Long after the feast had become a memory the Seven were assembled round the Master in the Aerie. The Master was silent as the companions reviewed the memorable events of that day. Some marvelled at the great outburst of enthusiasm with which the crowd received the Master's words. Others commented on Shamadam's odd and most inscrutable behaviour during the moments when scores of indebtedness bills were taken out of the Ark treasury and publicly destroyed, and hundreds of wine-jars and barrels brought out of the cellars and given away, and many valuable gifts returned to the givers; for he evinced no opposition whatsoever, as we all expected him to do, but speechless and motionless he watched it all weeping voluminous tears.

Bennoon remarked that though the crowd cheered itself hoarse, its cheers were not for the Master's words, but for the debts remitted and the gifts returned. He even mildly reproved the Master for wasting his breath on such a crowd which sought no higher pleasure than eating, drinking and making merry. The truth, he maintained, should not be preached indiscriminately to all, but to the chosen few. Then the Master spoke and said,

MIRDAD: Your breath upon the wind shall surely lodge within some breast. Ask not whose breast it is. See only that the breath itself be pure.

Your word shall seek and surely find some ear. Ask not whose ear it is. See only that the word itself be a true messenger of Freedom.

Your silent thought shall surely move some tongue to speech. Ask not whose tongue it is. See only that the thought itself be lit with loving Understanding.

Think not any effort wasted. Some seeds lie buried in the ground for many years, but quickly come to life when stirred by the breath of the first favouring season.

The seed of Truth is in all men and things. Your work is not to sow the Truth, but to prepare the favouring season for its springing up.

All things are possible in eternity, Therefore, despair of no man's freedom, but preach the message of release to all with equal faith and zeal – to the non-yearning as to the yearning. For the non-yearning shall surely come to yearn, and the now unfledged shall some day preen their pinions in the Sun, and with their wings shall cleave the farthest and the most inaccessible reaches of the sky.

*Micaster*: It grieves us much that till this day, and despite our repeated inquiries, the Master would not reveal to us the secret of his mysterious disappearance on the eve of the Day of the Vine. Are we not worthy of his confidence?

MIRDAD: Whoever is worthy of my love is surely worthy of my confidence. Is confidence more than Love, Micaster? Am I not giving you unstintingly of my heart?

If I spoke not of that unsavoury circumstance it was because I wished to give Shamadam time for repenting. For it was he, with the help of two strangers, who had forcefully taken me out of this Aerie on that eve and cast me into the Black Pit. Unhappy Shamadam! Little did he dream that even the Black Pit would receive Mirdad with silken hands and provide him with magic ladders to the summit.

*Naronda*: On hearing that we were all awestruck and dumbfounded, and none dared to ask the Master how he came out unscathed of what seemed to everyone a certain perdition. And all were silent for a space.

*Himbal*: Why does Shamadam persecute our Master while our Master loves Shamadam?

MIRDAD: Not me Shamadam persecutes, Shamadam persecutes Shamadam.

Invest the blind with a semblance of authority, and they will pluck the eyes of all the seeing, even the eyes of those who labour hard to make them see.

Give a slave his way but for a day, and he will turn the world into a world of slaves. The first he would flail and fetter would be the ones who toil incessantly to set him free.

All world authority, whatever be its source, is counterfeit. Therefore it clicks its spurs, and brandishes the sword, and rides in boisterous pomp and glittering ceremony that none may dare look into its false heart. Its shaky throne it mounts on guns and spears. Its vanity-swept soul it decorates with fear-inspiring amulets and necromantic emblems that the eyes of the curious may not behold its wretched poverty.

Such an authority is both a blind and a curse to the man who craves to exercise it. It would maintain itself at any cost, even the fearful cost of destroying the man himself and those who accept his authority, and those who oppose it as well.

Because of their lust for authority men are in constant turmoil. Those in authority are ever fighting to maintain it. Those out of authority are ever struggling to snatch it from the hands of those who hold it. While Man, the God in swaddling-bands, is trampled under foot and hoof and left on the field of battle unnoticed, unattended and unloved.

So furious is the fight, and so blood-crazed the fighters that none, alas, would stop to lift the painted mask off the face of the spurious bride and expose her monstrous ugliness to all.

Believe, O monks, that no authority is worth the flutter of an eyelash, except the authority of Holy Understanding which is priceless. For that no sacrifice is great. Attain it once, and you shall hold it to the end of Time. And it shall charge your words with more power than all the armies of the world can ever command; and it shall bless your deeds with more beneficence than all the world authorities combined can ever dream of bringing to the world.

For Understanding is its own shield; its strong arm is Love. It neither persecutes nor tyrannizes, but like unto dew it falls upon the arid hearts of men; and those who reject it it blesses no less than those who drink it in. Because too certain of its inner force, it has recourse to no external force. Because too fearless, it shuns the use of fear as a weapon for imposing itself on any man.

The world is poor – ah, so poor – in Understanding. Therefore does it seek to hide its poverty behind the veil of counterfeit authority. And counterfeit authority strikes defensive and offensive alliances with counterfeit force; and the two put Fear in command. And Fear destroys them both.

Has it not always been that the weak would combine to protect their weakness? Thus world's authority and world's brute force go hand in hand under the lash of Fear and pay their daily tax to Ignorance in wars and blood and tears And Ignorance benignly smiles on all and says to them, 'Well done!'

'Well done!' said Shamadam to Shamadam when he consigned Mirdad to the Pit. But little did Shamadam think that in casting me into the Pit he had cast himself, and not me. For the Pit cannot hold a Mirdad; while a Shamadam must labour long and hard to scale its dark and slippery walls.

A trinket is all world authority. Let those who are yet babes in Understanding amuse themselves with it. But you must not impose yourselves on any man. For that which is imposed by force is soon or late deposed by force.

Seek no authority over the lives of men; of that the Omniwill is master. Nor seek authority over the goods of men; for men are chained so much to their goods as to their lives, and they distrust and hate the meddlers with their chains. But seek a way into the hearts of men through Love and Understanding; and once installed therein you can the better work to loose men of their chains.

For Love will guide your hand, while Understanding holds the lantern.

# CHAPTER TWENTY-EIGHT

## Prince of Bethar
## Appears with Shamadam at the Aerie.
## The Colloquy between the Prince
## And Mirdad on War and Peace.
## Mirdad is trapped by Shamadam

*Naronda*: As the Master finished saying that, and we fell to pondering his words, heavy footfalls were heard outside accompanied by rambling, muffled talking. Presently two giant soldiers, armed to the teeth, appeared at the entrance and took positions on either side, with sabres drawn and glistening in the sun. Then followed a young prince in full regalia, with Shamadam timidly walking behind, and two more soldiers following Shamadam.

The prince was one of the most powerful and far famed potentates of the Milky Mountains. He stood for a moment at the entrance and carefully examined the faces of the small company assembled within. Then fixing his large and bright eyes on the Master, he bowed very low and said,

*Prince*: Hail, holy man! We came to do homage to the great Mirdad whose fame has travelled far in these mountains until it reached our distant capital.

MIRDAD: Fame rides a fiery chariot abroad. At home it limps on crutches. Of that the Senior is my witness. Trust not, O prince, to vagaries of fame.

*Prince*: Yet sweet are the vagaries of fame, and sweet it is to print one's name upon the lips of men.

MIRDAD: As well engrave a name upon the sands of the shore as print it on the lips of men. The winds and tides shall wash it off the sands. A sneeze shall blow it off the lip. If you would not be sneezed away by men, print not your name upon their lips, but burn it in their hearts.

*Prince*: But locked with many locks are the hearts of men.

MIRDAD: The locks may be many, but the key is one.

*Prince*: Have you that key? For I am in sore need of it.

MIRDAD: You, also, have it.

*Prince*: Alas! You price me for far more than I am really worth. Long have I sought a key into my neighbour's heart, but nowhere could I find it. He is a mighty prince and is bent on making war on me. And I am constrained to raise my arms against him despite my peaceful disposition. Let not my diadem and jewelled robes deceive you, Master. I cannot find in them the key I seek.

MIRDAD: They hide the key, but hold it not, They foil your step, and balk your hand, and lead away your eye, thus rendering your search of no avail.

*Prince*: What may the Master mean by that? Am I to cast away my diadem and robes that I may find the key into my neighbour's heart?

MIRDAD: To keep them you must lose your neighbour. To keep your neighbour you must lose them. And to lose one's neighbour is to lose oneself.

*Prince*: I would not buy my neighbour's friendliness at such a costly price.

MIRDAD: Would you not buy yourself at such a paltry price?

*Prince*: Buy myself? No prisoner am I to pay a ransom. And furthermore I have a well-paid, well-munitioned army to protect me. My neighbour cannot boast of a better one.

MIRDAD: To be the prisoner of one man, or thing, is alone imprisonment too bitter to endure. To be the prisoner of an army of men, and a host of things, is banishment without reprieve. For to depend on anything is to be imprisoned by that thing. Depend, therefore, on God alone. For to be the prisoner of God is to be free, indeed

*Prince*: Should I, then, leave myself, my throne, my subjects unprotected?

MIRDAD: You should not leave yourself unprotected.

*Prince*: Therefore do I maintain an army.

MIRDAD: Therefore must you dismiss your army.

*Prince*: But my neighbour would quickly overrun my kingdom.

MIRDAD: Your kingdom he may overrun. But you no man can swallow. Two prisons merged in one make not a tiny hearth for Freedom. Rejoice if any man expel you from your prison; but envy not that man who comes to shut himself within your prison.

*Prince*: I am the scion of a race famed for its valour in the field.

We never force on others war. But when war is forced upon us we never slink away, and never leave the field except with banners flying high over the corpses of the enemy. You ill advise me, sir, when you advise to let my neighbour have his way.

MIRDAD: Did you not say you would have peace?

*Prince*: Aye, peace would I have.

MIRDAD: Then do not fight.

*Prince*: But my neighbour insists on fighting me; and I must fight him that peace may reign between us.

MIRDAD: You would kill your neighbour that you may live with him at peace! How strange the spectacle! There is no merit in living at peace with the dead. But a great virtue it is to live at peace with the living. If you must wage a war on any living man, or thing, whose tastes and interests may clash at times with yours, then wage a war on God who caused these things to be. And wage a war upon the Universe; for countless are the things therein that disconcert your mind, and trouble your heart, and willy-nilly force themselves upon your life.

*Prince*: What should I do when I would be at peace with my neighbour, but he would fight?

MIRDAD: Fight!

*Prince*: Now you counsel me aright.

MIRDAD: Aye, fight! But not your neighbour. Fight rather all the things that cause you and your neighbour to fight.

Why does your neighbour wish to fight you? Is it because your eyes are blue, and his are hazel? Is it because you dream of angels, and he dreams of devils? Or is it because you love him as yourself and hold all yours as his?

It is your robes, O prince, your throne, your wealth, your glory and the things to which you are a prisoner that your neighbour wants to fight you for.

Would you defeat him without raising a spear against him? Then steal a march on him, and yourself declare a war on all these things. When you have conquered them by ridding your soul of their clutches; when you have cast them out upon the rubbish heap, mayhap your neighbour will halt his march, and sheath his sword, and say unto himself, 'Were these things worth a fight, my neighbour would not have cast them away upon the rubbish heap.'

Should your neighbour persevere in his madness and carry off the rubbish heap, rejoice at your own deliverance from such a noxious load, but grieve over your neighbour's lot.

*Prince*: What of my honour which is worth far more than all my possessions?

MIRDAD: Man's only honour is being Man, God's living likeness and image. All other honours are dishonours.

An honour bestowed by men is easily taken away by men. An honour written with the sword is easily effaced by the sword. No honour, O prince, is worth a rusted arrow; much less a burning tear; much less a drop of blood.

*Prince*: And freedom – my freedom and that of my people – is not that worth the greatest sacrifice?

MIRDAD: True Freedom is worth the sacrifice of self. Your neighbour's arms cannot take it away; your own arms cannot win it and defend it. And the field of battle is for it a grave.

True Freedom is won and lost in the heart.

Would you have war? Wage it within your heart upon your heart. Disarm your heart of every hope and fear and vain desire that make your world a stifling pen, and you shall find it broader than the Universe; and you shall roam that Universe at will; and nothing shall be unto you an hindrance.

That is the only war worth waging. Engage yourself in such a war, and you shall no longer find the time for any other wars which would become to you abhorrent beastliness and diabolic tricks meant to distract your mind, and sap your strength, and cause you thus to lose the great war with yourself which is indeed an holy war. To win that war is to win undying glory. But victory in any other war is worse than rank defeat. And that is the horror of all men's wars, that the victor and the vanquished equally espouse defeat.

Would you have peace? Look not for it in wordy documents; nor strive to grave it even in the rocks.

For the pen that scribbles 'Peace' with ease can scribble 'War' with equal ease; and the chisel that engraves 'Let us have peace' can easily engrave 'Let us have war.' And furthermore, the paper and the rock, and the pen and the chisel are soon attacked by moth, and rot, and rust, and all the alchemy of changing elements. Not so the timeless heart of Man which is the siege of Holy Understanding.

Once Understanding is unveiled, then victory is won and Peace established in the heart for ever and anon. An understanding heart is ever at peace even amid a war-dazed world.

An ignorant heart is a dual heart. A dual heart makes for a dual world. A dual world breeds constant strife and war.

Whereas an understanding heart is a single heart. A single heart makes for a single world. A single world is a world at peace. For it takes two to make a war.

Therefore do I counsel you to war upon your heart so as to make it single. The prize of victory is everlasting Peace.

When you can see, O prince, in any stone a throne; and find in any cave a castle, then too glad is the Sun to be your throne, and the constellations to be your castles.

When any daisy in the field is fit to serve you for a medal; and any worm to be for you a teacher, then joyful are the stars to pose upon your chest, and ready is the Earth to be your pulpit.

When you can rule your heart, what matters it to you who nominally rules your body? When all the Universe is yours, what matters it who has dominion over this or that tract of the Earth?

*Prince*: Your words are quite enticing. Yet does it appear to me that war is of Nature a law. Are not even the fishes of the sea in constant war? Is not the weak the prey of the strong? And I would not be anybody's prey.

MIRDAD: What appears to you as war is but a way of Nature to feed and propagate herself. The strong is made food for the weak no less than is the weak made food for the strong. Yet who is strong, and who is weak in Nature?

Nature alone is strong; all else are but weaklings obeying Nature's will and meekly flowing down the streams of Death.

The deathless only may be classed as strong. And Man is deathless, O prince. Aye, mightier than Nature is Man. He eats into her fleshy heart only to reach his fleshless heart. He propagates himself only to raise himself beyond self-propagation.

Let men who would be justified of their unclean desires by the clean instincts of the beast call themselves wild boars, or wolves, or jackals or what-not; but let them not debase the noble name of Man.

Believe Mirdad, O prince, and be at peace.

*Prince*: The Senior tells me that Mirdad is well-versed in the mysteries of witchcraft; and I would have him manifest some powers that I may believe in him.

MIRDAD: If unveiling God in Man be witchcraft, then is Mirdad a sorcerer. Do you desire of my sorcery a proof and a manifestation?

Behold, I am the proof and the manifestation.

Go to now. Do the work that you have come to do.

*Prince*: Well have you divined that I have other work to do than entertain my ears with your lunacies. For the prince of Bethar is a sorcerer of another sort; and anon he shall give a display of his art.

(To his men) Bring your chains and fetter up this God-Man, or Man-God, hands and feet, and let us show him and the present company what our sorcery is like.

*Naronda*: Like beasts of prey the four soldiers fell on the Master and quickly began to fasten chains about his hands and feet. For a moment the Seven sat paralysed, not knowing how to take what was going on before them – whether in jest or in earnest. Micayon and Zamora were quicker than the rest in realizing the earnestness of the ugly situation. They sprang upon the soldiers like two infuriated lions, and would have laid them low were it not for the restraining and reassuring voice of the Master.

MIRDAD: Let them ply their craft, impetuous Micayon. Let them have their way, good Zamora. No more appalling to Mirdad are their chains than was the Black Pit. Let Shamadam rejoice at patching his authority with that of the prince of Bethar. The patch shall rend them both.

*Micayon*: How shall we stand aside while our Master is being chained like a criminal?

MIRDAD: Have not the least anxiety for my sake. Be at Peace. So shall they do to you some day; but they shall harm themselves and not you.

*Prince*: So shall be done to every rogue and charlatan who dares to flout established right and authority.

This holy man (pointing to Shamadam) is the rightful head of this community, and his word must be law unto all. This sacred Ark whose bounties you enjoy is under my protection. My watchful eye surveys its destinies; my powerful arm is stretched over its roof and properties; my sword will clip the hand that would touch it with ill. Let all know that and beware.

(Again to his men) Lead this scoundrel out. His dangerous doctrine has well nigh ruined the Ark. It would soon ruin our kingdom and the earth if left to pursue its pernicious course. Let him from now on preach it to the grim walls of the dungeon of Bethar. Hence with him.

*Naronda*: The soldiers led the Master out, the prince and Shamadam following with gleeful pride. The Seven walked behind this ominous procession, their eyes following the Master, their lips glued with grief, their hearts bursting with tears.

The Master walked with a firm and certain step, and his head was lifted high. Having walked a distance, he looked back at us and said,

MIRDAD: Be steady in Mirdad. I shall not leave you till I launch my Ark and put you in command.

*Naronda*: And long thereafter did these words of his ring loud in our ears to the accompaniment of the heavy clanking of the chains.

# CHAPTER TWENTY-NINE

Shamadam vainly tries to win
The Companions over to himself
Mirdad miraculously returns
and gives all Companions, but Shamadam,
the Kiss of Faith

*Naronda*: Winter was upon us, abundant, white, and biting.

Voiceless and breathless stood the snow-wrapt mountains. Only the valleys below showed patches of faded green with here and there a band of fluid silver meandering towards the sea.

The Seven were buffeted about by alternating waves of hope and doubt. Micayon, Micaster and Zamora inclined to the hope that the Master would come back as he promised. Bennoon, Himbal and Abimar clung to their doubt of his return. But all felt a dreadful emptiness and a vexing futility.

The Ark was cold, and grim, and inhospitable. A frosty silence hung upon its walls despite Shamadam's tireless efforts to give it life and warmth. For ever since Mirdad was led away Shamadam sought to drown us with his kindliness. He offered us the best of food and wine; but the food did not sustain, and the wine did not enliven. He burned much wood and coal; but the fire did not give warmth. He was most polite and seemingly affectionate; but his politeness and affections estranged us from him more and more.

For long he made no mention of the Master. At length he opened up his heart and said,

*Shamadam*: You do me wrong, my companions, if you believe that I dislike Mirdad. Rather do I pity him with all my heart.

Mirdad may not be an evil man; but a dangerous visionary is he, and utterly impractical and false is the doctrine he holds forth in a world of hard facts and practices. He and those who follow him are headed for a tragic end at their first encounter with harsh reality. Of that I am very certain. And I would save my companions from such a catastrophe.

Mirdad may have a clever tongue inspired by the rashness of

youth; but his heart is blind and stubborn and ungodly. While I have the fear of the true God in my heart, and the experience of years to give my judgment weight and authority.

Who could have managed the Ark these many years to a better advantage than I? Have I not lived with you so long and been to you at once a brother and a father? Have not our minds been blessed with peace, and our hands with exceeding plenty? Why let a stranger demolish what we have been so long building, and sow distrust where trust was lord, and strife, where peace was king?

It is stark madness, my companions, to give up a bird in the hand for ten on the tree. Mirdad would have you give up this Ark which has sheltered you so long, and kept you near to God, and given you all that mortals can desire, and held you at a safe margin from the turmoil and anguish of the world. What does he promise you instead? Heartaches, and disappointments, and poverty with end-less strife to boot – that and many worse things does he promise you.

He promises an Ark in the air, in the vast nothingness – a mad-man's dream – a childish fantasy – a sweet impossibility. Is he, perchance, wiser than father Noah, the founder of the Mother-Ark? It pains me overmuch to have you give his ravings any thought.

I may have sinned against the Ark and its holy traditions when I appealed against Mirdad to the strong arm of my friend, the prince of Bethar. But I had your welfare at heart, and that alone should justify my transgression. I wished to save you and the Ark before it was too late. And God was with me, and I saved you.

Rejoice with me, companions, and thank the Lord for sparing us the great ignominy of seeing the undoing of our Ark with our sinful eyes. I, for one, could never outlive that shame.

But now I dedicate myself anew to the service of the God of Noah and his Ark, and your service, my beloved companions. Be happy as of yore that my happiness be complete in you.

*Naronda*: Shamadam wept as he said that, and his tears were pitiful because too lonely; for they found them no company in any of our hearts and eyes.

Of a certain morn, as the sun beamed out upon the mountains after a protracted siege of murky weather, Zamora took his harp and began to sing.

*Zamora*:

> Froze is the song on the frost-bitten lips
>    Of my harp.
> And ice-bound the dream in the ice-bound heart
>    Of my harp.
>
> Where is the breath that shall thaw out your song,
>    O my harp?
> Where is the hand that shall rescue the dream,
>    O my harp? –
>       In the dungeon of Bethar.
>
> Mendicant Wind, go and beg me a song
>    Of the chains
>       In the dungeon of Bethar.
> Sly rays of Sun, go and filch me a dream
> from the chains
>    Of the dungeon of Bethar.
>
> Sky-wide was spread of my eagle the wing,
>    And beneath it I was king.
> Now but a waif and an orphan am I,
>    And an owl rules my sky.
> For my eagle has flown to an aerie afar –
>       To the dungeon of Bethar.

*Naronda*: A tear dropped from Zamora's eye as his hands fell limp, and his head drooped low over the harp. That tear gave vent to our pent-up sorrow and opened up the sluices of our eyes.

Micayon jumped to his feet, and shouting with a loud voice 'I choke!', he made for the door and the open air. Zamora, Micaster and myself followed him through the court and to the gate in the great outer enclosure beyond which companions were not allowed to venture. Micayon drew the heavy bolt with one forceful jerk, flung the gate open and dashed out as a tiger from his cage. The other three followed Micayon.

The sun was warm and bright, and his rays, refracted on the frozen snow, were almost blinding. Treeless, snow-clad hills undulated before us so far as the eye could roam, and all seemed ablaze with fantastic hues of light. All about was a stillness so complete as to be ear-annoying; only the crunching snow beneath our feet broke the spell. The air, though nipping, so caressed our lungs that we felt as if borne onward without any effort on our part.

Even Micayon's mood was changed, and he stopped to exclaim, 'How good it is to be able to breathe. Ah, just to breathe!' And truly it seemed that for the first time we felt the joy of breathing freely and sensed the meaning of Breath.

We had walked a little way when Micaster espied a dark object on a far off eminence. Some thought it a lonely wolf; some, a rock swept clean of snow by the wind. But the object seemed to move in our direction, and we decided to lay our course towards it. Nearer and nearer it approached, assuming more and more a human shape. Suddenly Micayon took a great leap forward, shouting as he leapt, 'It is he! It is he!'

And he it was – his graceful gait, his stately bearing, his nobly lifted head. The light-hearted wind played hide-and-seek in his flowing garments and carelessly flirted his long, black locks. The sun had lightly tinged the delicate amber-brown of his face; but the dark and dreamy eyes scintillated as before and sent forth waves of confident serenity and triumphant love. His tender feet, strapped in wooden sandals, were kissed bright rose by the frost.

Micayon was the first to reach him; and he threw himself at his feet, sobbing, and laughing, and mumbling as one in delirium, 'Now is my soul restored unto me.'

The other three did likewise; but the Master raised them one by one, embracing each with infinite tenderness and saying as he embraced them,

MIRDAD: Receive the kiss of Faith. Henceforth you shall sleep in belief and rise in belief; and Doubt shall not nest in your pillow, nor paralyse your step with hesitation.

*Naronda*: The four who remained in the Ark, when they beheld the Master at the door thought him at first an apparition, and were much affrighted. But when he hailed them each by his name, and they heard his voice, they precipitated themselves to his feet, except Shamadam who remained glued to his seat. The Master did and said to the three as he had done and said to the four.

Shamadam blankly looked on and shook from head to feet, his face becoming deathly pale, his lips twitching, and his hands fumbling aimlessly at his belt. Suddenly he slipped off his seat, and crawling on all fours to where the Master stood, he put his arms around his feet and said convulsively with his face to the floor, 'I, too, believe.' The Master raised him also, but without kissing him said,

MIRDAD: It is Fear that shakes Shamadam's mighty frame and his tongue to say, 'I, too, believe.'

Shamadam trembles and bows before the 'witchery' that brought Mirdad out of the Black Pit and the dungeon of Bethar. And Shamadam fears retaliation. Let his mind be at ease on that score, and let him turn his heart in the direction of True Faith.

A faith that is borne upon a wave of Fear is but the foam of Fear; it rises and subsides with Fear. True Faith does not bloom save on the stalk of Love. Its fruit is Understanding. If you be afraid of God believe not in God.

*Shamadam*: (Drawing back, with his eyes always to the floor) A wretch and an outcast is Shamadam in his own house. Permit me, at least, to be your servant for a day and to bring you some meat and some warm clothing. For you must be very hungry and cold.

MIRDAD: I have meat unknown to kitchens, and warmth not borrowed from the thread of wool, or the tongue of fire. Would that Shamadam stored more of my meat and warmth and less of other victuals and combustibles.

Behold! The sea is come to winter on the peaks. And the peaks are glad to don the frozen sea as a coat. And the peaks are warm in their coat.

Glad also is the sea to lie for a space so still and so enchanted on the peaks; but only for a space. For Spring shall come, and the Sea, like a hibernating serpent, shall uncoil itself and reclaim its temporarily mortgaged freedom. And again it shall race from shore to shore; and again it shall mount the air, and roam the sky, and spray itself wherever it shall list.

But there be men like you, Shamadam, whose life is a constant winter and an unbroken hibernation. They are the ones who have received no omen yet of Spring. Behold! Mirdad is the omen. An omen of Life is Mirdad, and not a death-knell. How much longer would you hibernate?

Believe, Shamadam, that the life men live and the death they die are but a hibernation. And I am come to stir men from their sleep and call them out of their dens and holes unto the freedom of Life undying. Believe me for your sake and not for mine.

*Naronda*: Shamadam stood still and opened not his mouth. Bennoon whispered to me to ask the Master of how he contrived to escape from the dungeon of Bethar; but my tongue would not obey me to ask the question which, howbeit, was quickly divined by the Master.

MIRDAD: The dungeon of Bethar is no longer a dungeon. It has become a shrine. The prince of Bethar is no longer a prince. He is to-day a yearning pilgrim like you.

Even a gloomy dungeon, Bennoon, may be turned into a dazzling lighthouse. Even a haughty prince may be swayed to lay aside his crown before the crown of Truth. And even growling chains may be made to yield celestial music. Nothing is a miracle to Holy Understanding which is the only miracle.

*Naronda*: The Master's words concerning the abdication of the prince of Bethar fell like a stroke of lightning on Shamadam; and to our consternation he was suddenly seized with a spasm so strange and so violent that we seriously feared for his life. The spasm ended in a swoon, and we laboured long with him before we finally brought him to.

# CHAPTER THIRTY

## Micayon's Dream revealed by the Master

*Naronda*: For a long stretch before and after the Master's return from Bethar Micayon was observed to behave as one in trouble. He kept aloof most of the time, speaking little, eating little, and rarely leaving his cell. His secret he would not confide even to me. And we all marvelled that the Master would say or do nothing to assuage his pain, although he loved him very strongly.

Once, as Micayon with the rest were warming themselves round the brazier, the Master began to discourse on the Great Nostalgia.

MIRDAD: A certain man once had a dream. And this is the dream he had:

He saw himself upon the green bank of a broad, deep, and noiselessly flowing river. The bank was alive with great multitudes of men, women and children of every age and tongue; and all had wheels of various sizes and tints which they rolled up and down the bank. And the multitudes were dressed in festive colours, and were out to frolic and to feast; and their hubbub filled the air. Like a restless sea did they heave up and down, back and forth.

He alone was not dressed for the feast, for he was aware of no feast. And he alone had no wheel to roll. And hard as he strained his ear, he could not catch a single word from the polyglot crowd that was akin to his own dialect. And hard as he strained his eye, it could not rest upon a single face that was to it familiar. And further-more, the crowd, as it surged about him, cast meaningful glances in his direction as if to say, 'Who is this comical being?' Then it dawned in upon him that the feast was not his, and that he was a total stranger; and he felt a pang in his heart.

Anon he heard a great roar coming from the upper end of the bank, and forthwith he saw the multitudes fall to their knees, cover their eyes with their hands and bend their heads to the ground, breaking as they fell in two rows and leaving between an open, straight and narrow aisle all the length of the bank. He alone re-mained standing in the middle of the aisle not knowing what to do and which way to turn.

As he looked up to whence the roar was coming, he beheld an enormous bull spitting tongues of flame from his mouth and blowing columns of smoke from his nostrils, and dashing down the aisle at a lightning speed. In terror he looked at the furious beast, and sought escape right and left, but could find none. He felt as if transfixed to the ground, and was certain of his doom.

Just as the bull approached to where he felt the scorching flame and smoke the man was lifted in the air. The bull stood beneath him shooting more fire and smoke upward; but the man rose higher and higher, and though he felt the fire and the smoke, yet did he gain a certain confidence that the bull could no longer do him any harm. And he set his course across the river.

Looking down upon the green bank he saw the crowds still kneeling as before, and the bull shooting arrows at him instead of smoke and fire. He could hear the arrows hiss as they passed beneath him, some of them pierced his garments, but none did touch his flesh. At last the bull, the crowd and the river were out of sight; and the man flew on.

He flew over a dreary, sun-scorched land without any trace of life whatsoever. At length he alighted at the foot of a high, rugged mountain desolate not only of a blade of grass, but even of a lizard and an ant. And he felt as though his only road lay up the mountain.

Long did he look for a safe way up, but all he could see was a barely traceable trail such as goats only can walk. That trail he decided to follow.

Scarce had he risen a few hundred feet when he saw, not far to his left, a broad and a smooth roadbed. As he stopped and was about to leave his trail the roadbed became a human stream, one half of it laboriously ascending, the other rushing headlong down the mountain. Men and women in untold numbers struggled up and rolled down, head over heels, and sent forth as they rolled down such moans and groans as to strike terror in the heart.

The man observed this weird phenomenon for a while and decided in his mind that somewhere up the mountain was an immense madhouse, and that those rolling down were some of its escaped inmates. And he continued on his winding trail, falling here and rising there, but always winding higher and higher.

At a certain height the human stream dried up, and its bed became entirely effaced. Again the man was alone with the sombre mountain, and no hand to point the way, and no voice to bolster up his waning courage and steel his rapidly failing strength, excepting a vague belief that his course lay towards the summit.

On and on he plodded tracing his path with his blood. After much soul-rending toil he arrived at a spot where the earth was soft and stoneless. To his indescribable delight he saw some delicate tufts of grass sprouting here and yon; and the grass was so tender, and the soil so velvety, and the air so aromatic and so lulling that he felt as one robbed of the last ounce of strength. So he relaxed and fell asleep.

He was awakened by a hand touching his hand and a voice saying to him, 'Arise! The summit is in sight. And Spring awaits you on the summit.'

The hand and the voice were those of a most beauteous maiden – a paradisic being – dressed in a robe of dazzling whiteness. She gently took the man by the hand; and the man arose invigorated and refreshed. And the man did glimpse the summit. And the man did smell the Spring. But just as he raised his foot to take the first step forward he awoke from his dream.

What would Micayon do were he to awaken from such a dream and find him stretched upon a common bed, hemmed in within four common walls, but with the vision of that maiden glowing behind his eyelids, and the fragrant effulgence of that summit fresh in his heart?

*Micayon*: (As if stung) But I am that dreamer, and mine is that dream. Mine also is the vision of that maiden and the summit. It haunts me till this day and gives me no repose. It made me a stranger to myself. Because of it Micayon no longer knows Micayon.

Yet I dreamed that dream soon after you were led away to Bethar. How come you relate it in such minute details? What manner of man are you that even dreams of men are to you an open book?

Ah, the freedom of that summit! Ah, the beauty of that maiden! How trite is all else in comparison. My very soul has deserted me for their sake. And only on that day when I saw you coming from Bethar did my soul rejoin me, and I felt calm and strong. But the feeling has left me since, and again am I drawn away from myself by threads invisible.

Save me, O my Great Companion. I languish away for a vision.

MIRDAD: You know not what you ask, Micayon. Would you be saved from your saviour?

*Micayon*: I would be spared this unendurable torture of being so homeless in a world so snug at home. I would be on the summit with the maiden.

MIRDAD: Rejoice because your heart has been seized with the Great Nostalgia; for that is a promise irrevocable that you shall find your country and your home, and be upon the summit with the maiden.

*Abimar*: Pray, tell us more of this Nostalgia. By what symptoms may we recognize it?

# CHAPTER THIRTY-ONE

# The Great Nostalgia

MIRDAD: Like mist is the Great Nostalgia. Emitted by the heart, it shuts away the heart, as mist, effused by sea and land, obliterates both land and sea.

And also as the mist bereaves the eye of visible reality making itself the sole reality, so this Nostalgia subdues the feelings of the heart and makes itself the feeling paramount. And seemingly so formless, and aimless, and blind as the mist, yet like the mist it teems with forms unborn, is clear of sight and very definite of purpose.

Like fever also is the Great Nostalgia. As fever, ignited in the body, saps the vitality of the body while burning up its poisons, so this Nostalgia, born of the friction in the heart, debilitates the heart, as it consumes away its dross and every superfluity.

And like a thief is the Great Nostalgia. For as a sneaking thief relieves his victim of a burden, yet leaves him sore embittered, so this Nostalgia, by stealth, lifts all the burdens of the heart, yet leaves it most disconsolate and burdened by its very lack of burdens.

Broad is the bank and green where men and women dance away, and sing away, and toil and weep away their evanescent days. But fearsome is the fire-and-smoke-belching Bull that hobbles up their feet, and brings them to their knees, and stuffs back their songs into their vocal chords, and glues their swollen eyelids with their tears.

Broad also and deep is the stream that separates them from the other bank. And neither can they swim it, nor can they row across it with an oar, nor sail it with a sail. Few – very few – of them venture to span it with a thought. But all – almost all – are eager to adhere to their bank where each goes on rolling his pet wheel of Time.

The man with the Great Nostalgia has no pet wheel to roll. Amid a world so tensely occupied and pressed for time he is alone without an occupation and unhurried. In a humanity so decorous in dress, and speech, and manner he finds him naked, stuttering and awkward.

He cannot laugh with the laughing, nor can he with the weeping weep: Men eat and drink, and have pleasure in eating and drinking; he eats without a relish, and his drink is vapid in his mouth.

Others are mated, or busy seeking mates; he walks alone, and sleeps alone, and dreams his dreams alone. Others are rich in wordly wit and wisdom; he alone is dull and unwise. Others have cosy corners which they call homes; he alone is homeless. Others have certain spots of the earth which they call native land and whose glory they sing very loud; he alone has no spot to sing and to call his native land. For his heart's eye is towards the other bank.

A sleepwalker is the man with the Great Nostalgia amid a world apparently so wide awake. He is drawn by a dream which those about him neither see nor feel; therefore they shrug their shoulders and titter in their sleeves. But when the god of Fear – the fire-and-smoke-belching Bull – appears on the scene, then are they made to bite the dust while the sleepwalker at whom they shrugged their shoulders and tittered in their sleeves is lifted on the wings of Faith above them and their bull, and carried far over the other bank and to the foot of the Rugged Mountain.

Barren, and bleak, and forlorn is the land over which the somnambulist flies. But the wings of Faith are strong; and the man flies on.

Sombre, and bald, and blood-curdling the mountain at whose foot ne descends. But the heart of Faith is indomitable; and the man's heart boldly beats on.

Rocky, and slippery, and barely discernible his trail up the mountain. But silken is the hand, and steady is the foot, and keen is the eye of Faith, and the man climbs on.

He meets on the way with men and women labouring up the mountain along a broad and a smooth roadbed. They are the men and women of the Small Nostalgia who crave to reach the summit, but with a lame and a sightless guide. For their guide is their belief in what the eye can see, and what the ear can hear, and what the hand can feel, and what the nose and tongue can smell and taste. Some of them rise no higher than the mountain's ankles; some reach its knees; and some the hips; and very few the girdle. But all slip back with their guide and go tumbling down the mountain without so much as glimpsing the fair summit.

Can the eye see all to be seen, and the ear hear all to be heard? Can the hand feel all to be felt, and the nose smell all to be smelled? Or can the tongue taste all to be tasted? Only when Faith, born of divine Imagination, comes to their aid will the senses truly sense and thus become ladders to the summit.

Senses devoid of Faith are most undependable guides. Though their road appear to be smooth and broad, yet is it full of hidden traps and pitfalls; and those who take it to the summit of Freedom either perish on the way, or slip and tumble back to the base from which they made their start; and there they nurse many a broken bone; and there they stitch many a gaping wound.

The men with the Small Nostalgia are they who, having built a world with their senses, soon find it small and stuffy; and so they long for a larger and airier home. But instead of seeking new materials and a new master builder, they rummage up the old materials and call upon the same architect – the senses – to design and build for them the larger home. No sooner is the new one built than they find it so small and so stuffy as the old. And so they go on demolishing and building and never can they build the home that gives them the comfort and the freedom they crave. For they rely upon their deceivers to save them from deceit. And like the fish that jumps from the frying pan into the fire, they run away from a small mirage only to be lured by a bigger one.

Between the men of the Great and the men of the Small Nostalgia are the vast herds of rabbit-men who feel no nostalgia at all. They are content to dig their holes and live and breed and die therein; and they find their holes quite elegant, and roomy, and warm, and would not exchange them for the splendours of a kingly palace. And they snicker at all somnambulists, especially the ones who walk a solitary trail where footprints are few and very hard to trace.

Much like an eagle hatched by a backyard hen and cooped up with the brood of that hen is the man with the Great Nostalgia among his fellow-men. His brother-chicks and mother-hen would have the young eagle as one of them, possessed of their nature and habits, and living as they live; and he would have them like himself – dreamers of the freer air and skies illimitable. But soon he finds him a stranger and a pariah among them; and he is pecked by all – even his mother. But the call of the summits is loud in his blood, and the stench of the coop exasperating to his nose. Yet does he suffer it all in silence till he is fully fledged. And then he mounts the air, and casts a loving farewell look upon his erstwhile brothers and their mother who merrily cackle on as they dig in the earth for more seed and worms.

Rejoice, Micayon. Yours is a prophet's dream. The Great Nostalgia has made your world too small, and made you a stranger in that world. It has unloosed your imagination from the grip of the despotic senses; and imagination has brought you forth your Faith.

And Faith shall lift you high above the stagnant, stifling world and carry you across the dreary emptiness and up the Rugged Mountain where every faith must needs be tried and purified of the last dregs of Doubt.

And Faith so purified and triumphant shall lead you to the boundaries of the eternally green Summit and there deliver you into the hands of Understanding. Having discharged its task, Faith shall retire, and Understanding shall guide your steps to the unutterable Freedom of the Summit which is the true, the boundless, the all-including home of God and the Overcoming Man.

Stand well to the test, Micayon. Stand well, you all. To stand but for a moment on that summit is worth enduring every kind of pain. But to abide forever on that Summit is worth Eternity.

*Himbal*: Would you not lift us now to your summit though for a glimpse, however brief?

MIRDAD: Be not in haste, Himbal, and bide your time. Where I breathe freely, there you gasp for breath. Where I walk lightly, there you pant and stumble. Keep your hold on Faith; and Faith shall perform the gigantic feat.

So taught I Noah.

So I teach you.

## CHAPTER THIRTY-TWO

# On Sin and the Shedding
## of the Fig-Leaf Aprons

MIRDAD: You have been told of Sin, and you would know how Man became a sinner.

And you declare – and not without a merit – that if Man, the image and the likeness of God, be a sinner, then God Himself must be the source of Sin. Therein is a snare for the unsuspecting; and I would not have you, my companions, ensnared. Therefore would I remove this snare from your path that you may remove it from the paths of men.

There is no sin in God, unless it be sin for the Sun to give of his light to a candle. Nor is there sin in Man, unless it be sin for a candle to burn itself away in the Sun and thus be joined unto the Sun.

But there is sin in the candle that would not give forth its light, and when a match is applied to its wick, it curses the match and the hand that applied it. There is sin in the candle that is *ashamed* of burning in the Sun; therefore would screen itself away from the Sun.

Man did not sin by disobeying the Law; rather by covering his ignorance of the Law.

Aye, there is sin in the fig-leaf apron.

Have you not read the story of the *fall* of Man, so frugal and naive of word, but so sublime and so subtle of meaning? Have you not read how Man, when fresh from the bosom of God, was like an infant God – passive, inert, uncreative? For though endowed with all the attributes of godhood yet, like all infants, was he incapable of knowing, much less of exercising, his infinite capacities and talents.

Like a lonely seed enclosed in a beauteous vial was Man in the garden of Eden. A seed in a vial will remain a seed, and never will the marvels sealed up within its skin be stirred to life and light save it be hid in a soil congenial to its nature, and the skin thereof be broken.

But Man had no soil of his nature to plant himself therein and to sprout forth.

152

## On Sin and the Shedding of the Fig-Leaf Aprons

His was a face nowhere reflected in a kindred face. His was a human ear which heard no human voice. His was a human voice which echoed back from no human throat. His was a heart which beat a lonely unison.

Alone – so utterly alone – was Man amid a world well paired and launched upon its course. He was a stranger to himself; he had no labour of his own and no set course to follow. Eden to him was what a comfortable crib is to a babe – a state of passive bliss; a well-appointed incubator.

The tree of the knowledge of Good and Evil, and the tree of Life were both within his reach; yet would he stretch no hand to pluck and taste of their fruit; for his taste and his will, his thoughts and his desires, and even his very life were all wrapped up within him and awaiting to be slowly unwrapped. He, by himself, could not do the unwrapping. Therefore was he made to yield out of himself a *helpmeet* for himself – a hand that would help him unwind his many wrappings.

Where else could his help be got save from his own being so rich with help because so potent with divinity? And that is most significant.

Not a new dust and breath is Eve; but the very dust and breath of Adam – a bone of his bone and a flesh of his flesh. Not another creature appears on the scene; but the self-same single Adam is made a twain – a He-Adam and a She-Adam.

Thus the solitary, unmirrored face acquires a companion and a mirror; and the name unechoed in any human voice begins to reverberate in sweet refrains up and down the alleys of Eden; and the heart whose lonely beats were muffled in a lonely breast begins to feel its pulse and to hear its beats in a companion heart within a companion breast.

Thus the sparkless steel encounters the flint which brings forth its sparks in abundance. Thus the unlit candle is set a-light from both ends.

One is the candle, one is the wick, and one is the light, though issuing from seemingly opposite ends. And thus the seed in the vial finds the soil where it can germinate and unfold its mysteries.

So does Unity unconscious of itself beget Duality, that through the friction and the opposition of Duality it may be made to understand its unity. In that also is Man the faithful image and the likeness of his God. For God – the Primal Consciousness – projects of Himself the Word; and both Word and Consciousness are unified in Holy Understanding.

Not a punishment is Duality, but a process inherent in the nature of Unity and necessary for the unfolding of its divinity. How childish to think otherwise! How childish to believe that so stupendous a process can be made to run its course in three-score years and ten, or even in three-score millions of years!

Is it so small a matter to become a god?

Is God so cruel and so miserly a taskmaster that, with all eternity to give away, He should allot Man no more than so brief a span as seventy years in which to unify himself and to regain his Eden fully aware of his godhood and his unity with God?

Long is the course of Duality; and foolish are they who would measure it with calendars. Eternity counts not the revolutions of the stars.

When Adam the passive, the inert, the uncreative was made dual he forthwith became active, full of motion and able to create and to procreate himself.

What was the first act of Adam made dual? It was *to eat* of the tree of the knowledge of Good and Evil and thus to make his whole world as dual as himself. No longer were things what they were – innocent and indifferent. But they became either good or bad, useful or harmful, pleasant or unpleasant; they became two opposing camps, whereas before they were one.

And the serpent that *beguiled* Eve to taste of Good and Evil, was he not the deeper voice of active, yet inexperienced, Duality urging itself to act and to experience?

That Eve was the first to hear that voice and to obey it is no wonder at all. For Eve was the whetstone, as it were; the instrument designed to bring out the powers latent in her mate.

Have you not often stopped to visualize this first Woman in this first human story stealing her way among the trees of Eden, her nerves on edge, her heart a-flutter like a bird in a cage, her eyes searching everywhere for possible detection, her mouth watering as her trembling hand reached out for the tempting fruit? Have you not held your breath as she plucked the fruit and sunk her teeth into its tender meat to taste a momentary sweetness which was to turn to everlasting bitterness for herself and all her progeny?

Have you not wished with all your hearts that God would forestall Eve's insane audacity by appearing to her just as she was about to commit her reckless deed, and not afterward as He does in the story? And having committed her deed, have you not wished that Adam would possess the wisdom and the courage to abstain from being her accomplice?

Yet neither did God intervene, nor Adam abstain. For God would not have His likeness unlike Him. It was His will and *plan* that Man should walk the long way of Duality in order to unfold his own will and plan and unify himself by Understanding. As to Adam he could not, even if he wished, refrain from partaking of the fruit tendered him by his wife. It was incumbent on him to eat of it simply because his wife had eaten of it, for the two were one flesh, and each was accountable for the other's acts.

Was God indignant and wroth because Man ate of the fruit of Good and Evil? God forbid. For He knew that Man could not but eat, and He wished him to eat; but He wished him also to know beforehand the consequence of eating and to have the stamina to face that consequence. And Man had the stamina. And Man did eat. And Man faced the consequence.

And the consequence was Death. For Man in becoming actively dual through the will of God had forthwith died to passive unity. Therefore is Death no penalty, but a phase of life inherent in Duality. For the nature of Duality is to make all things dual and to beget for everything a shadow. So Adam begot his shadow in Eve; and both begot for their life a shadow called Death. But Adam and Eve, though shadowed by Death, continue to have shadowless life in the life of God.

A constant friction is Duality; and the friction gives the illusion of two opposing sides bent upon self-extermination. In truth the seeming opposites are self-completing, self-fulfilling and working hand in hand to one and the same end – the perfect peace, and unity, and balance of Holy Understanding. But the illusion is rooted in the senses, and it persists so long as the senses persist.

Therefore did Adam answer God when He called him after *his eyes were opened*, 'I heard thy voice in the garden, and *I* was afraid because *I* was naked; and *I* hid myself.' Also, 'The woman thou gavest to be with *me*, she gave *me* of the tree, and *I* did eat.'

No other was Eve but Adam's very bone and very flesh. Yet consider this new-born *I* of Adam which, after its eyes were *opened*, began to see itself as something different, apart, and independent of Eve, of God and of all God's creation.

An illusion was this *I*. An illusion of the newly *opened* eye was this personality detached from God. It had nor substance, nor reality. It was born that through its death Man might come to know his real self which is the self of God. It shall vanish away when the outer eye is darkened and the inner eye is illumined. And though it baffled Adam, yet did it strongly intrigue his mind and lure his imagination. To have a self which one can call entirely one's own – that is indeed too flattering and too tempting to Man who has no consciousness of any self.

And Adam was tempted and flattered by his illusory self. And though he was *ashamed* of it because too unreal, or too *naked*, yet would he not part therewith; instead he clung to it with all his heart and all his new-born ingenuity. And he sewed fig leaves together and made him an apron wherewith to cover up his *naked* personality and keep it to himself away from the all-penetrating eye of God.

So Eden, the state of blissful innocence, the unity unconscious of itself, fell away from the dual fig-leaf aproned Man; and swords of flame were put between him and the Tree of Life.

Man walked out of Eden through the twin gate of Good and Evil; he shall walk in through the single gate of Understanding. He made his exit with his back to the Tree of Life; he shall re-enter with his face to that Tree. He set out on his long and trying journey ashamed of his nakedness and careful to hide his shame; he shall reach his journey's end with his purity unaproned, and with his heart proud of his nudity.

But that shall not come to pass till Man by *Sin* be delivered from *Sin*. For Sin shall prove its own undoing. And where is Sin but in the fig-leaf apron?

Aye, nothing else is Sin but the barrier that Man set up between himself and God – between his transient self and his abiding Self.

At first but a handful of fig leaves, that barrier has come to be a mighty bulwark. For ever since he shed away the innocence of Eden Man has been very hard at work amassing more and more fig leaves and sewing aprons upon aprons.

The slothful are content to go on patching up the rents in their aprons with shreds discarded by their more industrious neighbours. And every patch in the garment of Sin is sin, for it tends to perpetuate that shame which was Man's first and very poignant feeling upon his detachment from God.

Is Man doing aught to overcome his shame? Alas! All his labours are shame heaped up on shame, and aprons upon aprons.

What are Man's arts and learnings but fig leaves?

His empires, nations, racial segregations and religions on the war path, are they not cults of fig-leaf worship?

His codes of right and wrong, of honour and dishonour, of justice and injustice; his countless social creeds and conventions – are they not fig-leaf aprons?

His valuing the invaluable, and measuring the immeasurable, and standardizing what is beyond any standard – is not all that patching the overpatched loin-cloth?

His gluttony for pleasures that are rife with pain; his greed for riches that empoverish; his thirst for mastery that subjugates, and lust for grandeur that belittles – are not all these so many figleaf aprons?

In his pathetic rush to cover up his *nakedness* Man has put on too many aprons which in the course of years have stuck so tightly to his skin that he no longer distinguishes between them and his skin. And Man gasps for breath; and Man appeals for relief from his many skins. Yet, in his delirium, Man would do all things to be relieved of his burden except the only thing that can in truth relieve him of his burden, and that is to throw off that burden. He would be rid of his extra skins while clinging to them with all his might. He would be denuded, and yet remain fully dressed.

The time of denuding is at hand. And I am come to help you shed away your extra skins – your fig-leaf aprons – that you may help all yearners in the world to shed away theirs, too. I only point the way; but each shall do his shedding by himself, however painful be the undertaking.

Wait not on any miracle to save you from yourself, nor be afraid of pain; for naked Understanding shall turn your pain into an ever-lasting ecstasy of joy.

Should you then face yourselves in the nakedness of Understanding, and should God call to you and ask: 'Where are you?', you would not feel ashamed; nor would you be afraid; nor would you hide away from God. But rather would you stand unshaken, unbound, and divinely serene, and answer back to God:

'Behold us, God – our soul, our being, our only self. In shame, and fear and pain have we walked the long, and rough, and tortuous path of Good and Evil which you have appointed us at the dawn of Time. The Great Nostalgia urged our feet, and Faith sustained our hearts, and now has Understanding lifted our burdens, bound up our wounds, and brought us back into your holy presence naked of Good and Evil, Life and Death; naked of all illusions of Duality; naked of every self except your all-embracing Self. With no fig leaves to hide our nakedness we stand before you unashamed, illumined, unafraid. Behold, we are unified. Behold, we have overcome.'

And God shall embrace you with infinite Love, and straightway shall lead you unto His Tree of Life.

So taught I Noah.

So I teach you.

*Naronda*: This also was said by the Master around the brazier.

# CHAPTER THIRTY-THREE

## On Night – The Peerless Singer

*Naronda*: As longs an exile for his hearth so longed we all for the Aerie which icy winds and heavy snowdrifts had rendered inaccessible the winter long.

The Master chose a night of Spring whose eyes were soft and bright, whose breath was warm and aromatic, whose heart was quick and wide-awake in which to lead us to the Aerie.

The eight flat stones which served us for seats were still arranged in the self-same semi-circle as when we left them on the day the Master was led to Bethar. It was evident that none had visited the Aerie since that day.

Each of us took his usual seat and waited on the Master to speak. But he would not open his mouth. Even the full moon looking in upon us, as if to bid us welcome, seemed to hang in suspense upon the Master's lips.

Mountain cataracts, tumbling from crag to crag, filled the night with their boisterous melodies. Occasionally the hooting of an owl, or the broken notes of a cricket's song would find their way into our ears.

Long did we wait in breathless silence before the Master raised his head, and opening his half-shut eyes, began to speak to us in this wise:

MIRDAD: In the stillness of this night Mirdad would have you hear the songs of Night. Give ear unto the choir of Night. For verily is Night a peerless singer.

Out of the darkest crannies of the past; out of the brightest castles of the future; from the pinnacles of heavens and the bowels of the earth Night's voices gush and rush unto the farthest corners of the universe. In mighty waves they roll and eddy round your ears. Unburden well your ears that you may hear them well.

What bustling Day nonchalantly blots out, unhurried Night restores with passing wizardry. Do not the moon and stars hide in the glare of Day? What Day drowns out in hodge-podge make-believe, Night chants abroad in measured ecstasy. Even the dreams of herbs swell up the choir of Night.

Lend your ears to the spheres:
As they swing through the skies
Hear them sing lullabies
To the giant babe aslumber
In a cradle of quicksands,
To the king in pauper's tatters,
To the lightning held in fetters –
To the god in swaddling bands.

Hear the Earth, at once in travail,
Suckling, rearing, marrying, burying.
In the forest wild beasts prowling,
Growling, howling, tearing, torn;
Creepers pursuing their ways;
Insects humming mystic lays;
Birds rehearsing in their dreams
Tales of meadows, songs of streams;
Trees and shrubs and every breath
Quaffing life in cups of death.

From the summit and the vale;
From the desert and the sea;
From the air and from beneath the sod
Rolls out the challenge to the Time-veiled God.

Hear the mothers of the world –
How they weep, how they wail;
And the fathers of the world –
How they moan, how they groan.
Hear their sons and daughters run
To the gun and from the gun,
Scolding God and cursing Fate.
Feigning love and breathing hate,
Drinking zeal and sweating fears,
Sowing smiles and reaping tears,
Whetting with their crimson blood
The fury of the gathering flood.

Hear their famished bellies shrink,
And their swollen eyelids blink,

And their withered fingers grope
For the carcass of their hope;
And their hearts distend and crack
Heap on heap, and stack on stack.

Hear the fiendish engines rumble,
And the haughty cities tumble,
And the mighty citadels
Peal away their own death knells;
And the monuments of yore
Splash in pools of mud and gore.

Hear the prayers of the just
Chime along with shrieks of lust,
And the infant's artless prattle
Rhapsodize with wicked tattle,
And the maiden's blushing smile
Warble with the harlot's guile,
And the rapture of the brave
Hum the broodings of the knave.

In every tent and hut of every tribe and clan
Night trumpets forth the battle hymn of Man.

But Night, the sorceress, blends well the lullabies,
The challenges, the battle hymns and all
Into a song too subtle for the ear –
A song so grand, so infinite in sweep,
So deep of tone, so mellow of refrain
That even angels' choirs and symphonies
Are noise and babble in comparison.
That is the Overcomer's triumph song.

The mountains drowsing in the lap of Night,
The reminiscent deserts with their dunes,
The deeps somnambulant, the roving stars,
The dwellers in the cities of the dead,
The Holy Triad and the Omniwill
Hail and acclaim the Overcoming Man.
Happy are they who hear and understand.

Happy are they who, when alone with Night,
Feel calm, and deep, and broad as Night;
Whose faces are not smitten in the dark by wrongs
They perpetrated in the dark;
Whose eyelids do not smart with tears they caused
Their fellowmen to shed;
Whose hands do not itch with mischief and with greed;
Whose ears are not besieged with hissings of their lusts;
Whose thoughts are not bitten with their thoughts;
Whose hearts are not hives for all manner of cares
That swarm without an end from every nook of Time;
Whose fears burrow no tunnels in their brains;
Who can say boldly unto Night, 'Reveal us unto Day',
And say to Day, 'Reveal us unto Night'.
Aye, thrice happy are they who, when alone with Night,
Feel so well-tuned, so still, so infinite as Night.
To them alone Night sings the Overcomer's song.

If you would face the calumny of Day with heads aloft and eyes alight with faith, hasten to win the friendliness of Night.

Be friends with Night. Wash thoroughly your hearts in your own life blood and place them in her heart. Entrust your naked yearnings to her bosom, and immolate ambitions at her feet save the ambition to be free through Holy Understanding. Then shall you be invulnerable to all the shafts of Day, and Night shall bear you witness before men that you in truth are overcomers.

Though feverish days toss you hither and yon,
And starless nights enfold you in their gloom,
And you be cast upon the world's crossroads,
With no footprints or signs to show the way,
Yet would you fear no man or circumstance,
And would you have no shadow of a doubt
That days and nights, as well as men and things
Would seek you soon or late and meekly beg you
To command them.
For you have gained the confidence of Night.
And he who gains the confidence of Night
Can easily command the coming day.

## On Night – the Peerless Singer

Give ear unto the heart of Night, for in it beats the Overcomer's heart.

If I had tears I'd offer them to-night to every twinkling star and speck of dust; to every gurgling brook and singing katydid; to every violet wafting on the air its fragrant soul; to every racing wind; to every mount and vale; to every tree and every blade of grass – to all the passing peace and beauty of this Night, I'd pour my tears before them as apologies for men's ingratitude and savage ignorance.

For men, the conscripts of the heinous Penny, are busy in the service of their lord, too busy to give heed to any voice and will except his voice and will.

And dreadful is the business of men's lord. It is to turn their world into a slaughter-house wherein they are the butchers and the butchered. And so, inebriate with gore, men slaughter men in the belief that he who slaughters more falls heir to all the shares of those he slaughtered in all the bounties of the earth and the munificence of the skies.

Unhappy dupes! When did a wolf ever become a lamb by tearing up another wolf? When did a snake ever become a dove by crushing and devouring fellow-snakes? When did a man, by killing other men, inherit but their joys without their sorrows? When did an ear, by plugging other ears, become better attuned to harmonies of Life? Or did an eye, by plucking other eyes, become more sensitive to Beauty's emanations?

Is there a man, or any host of men, who can exhaust the blessings of a single hour whether of bread and wine, whether of light and peace? The Earth does not give birth to more than she can feed. The skies solicit not, nor steal subsistence for their young.

They lie who say to men, 'If you would have your fill, kill and inherit those you kill'.

How shall he prosper on the tears and blood and agonies of men who failed to prosper on their love, and on the milk and honey of the Earth, and on the deep affections of the skies?

They lie who say to men, 'Each nation for itself'.

How could a centipede ever advance an inch if each leg were to move in contrary direction to the others, or block the progress of the others, or plot destruction for the others? Is not mankind a monster centipede whose many legs are nations?

They lie who say to men, 'To rule is honour, to be ruled is shame'. Is not a donkey driver led by his donkey's tail? Is not a jailer bound unto the jailed?

Verily the donkey drives his leader; the jailbird jails his jailer.

They lie who say to men, 'The race is to the swift, the right is to the mighty'.

For life is not a race of muscle and of brawn. The cripple and the maimed too often reach the goal much quicker than the whole. And even a gnat sometimes lays low a gladiator.

They lie who say to men that wrong cannot be righted save with wrong. A wrong superimposed upon another wrong will never make a right. Let wrong alone, and it will work its own undoing,

But men are gullible of all their lord's philosophy. The Penny and his cormorants they piously believe and faithfully fulfil their wildest vagaries. While Night that sings and preaches of deliverance – and even God Himself – they neither trust nor heed. And you, companions, shall they brand either as lunatics or as imposters.

Take no offence at men's ingratitude and stinging mockery; but labour with a love and patience inexhaustible for their deliverance from themselves and from the flood of fire and blood that shall be soon upon them.

'Tis time men stopped the butchering of men.

The sun and moon and stars are since eternity awaiting to be seen and heard and understood; the alphabet of Earth, to be deciphered; the highways of Space, to be travelled; the ravelled thread of Time, to be unravelled; the fragrance of the universe, to be inhaled; the catacombs of Pain, to be demolished; the den of Death, to be ransacked; the bread of Understanding, to be tasted; and Man, the God in veils, to be unveiled.

'Tis time men stopped the pillaging of men and unified their ranks to carry on the common task. Enormous is the task, but sweet the victory. All else is trite and empty in comparison.

Yea, it is time. But few only shall heed. The others must await another call – another dawn.

# CHAPTER THIRTY-FOUR

## On the Mother Ovum

MIRDAD: In the stillness of this night Mirdad would have you meditate upon the Mother Ovum.

Space and all therein is an ovum whose shell is Time. That is the Mother Ovum.

Enveloping this Ovum, as air envelops the Earth, is God *Evolved*, the *Macro*-God, Life unembodied, infinite and ineffable.

Enveloped in this Ovum is God *Involved*, the *Micro*-God, Life embodied, and likewise infinite and ineffable.

Though measureless as human measures go, yet has the Mother Ovum bourns. While not infinite itself, it borders on infinity on every side.

All things and beings in the universe are nothing more than space-time ova enclosing the same *Micro*-God, but in varying stages of unfolding. The *Micro*-God in Man has a greater space-time expansion than the *Micro*-God in the animal; and that in the animal a greater expansion than that in the plant, and so on down the scale of creation.

The countless ova representing all things and beings, visible and invisible, are so arranged within the Mother Ovum that the larger in expansion contains the immediately smaller, with spaces intervening, down to the smallest ovum which is the central nucleus enclosed in space and time *infinitesimal*.

An ovum within an ovum, within an ovum, defying human numbers, and all God-fertilized – that is the universe, my companions.

Yet do I feel my words too slippery for your minds, and fain would make them safe and steady rungs, were any words ever made safe and steady rungs in the ladder that leads to perfect Understanding. Hang on to more than words and by more than your minds, if you would reach the heights and depths and breadths Mirdad would have you reach.

Words, at best, are flashes that reveal horizons; they are not the way to those horizons; still less are they those horizons. So when I speak to you of The Ovum and ova, and of *Macro*-God and *Micro*-God, hang not unto the letter, but follow the flash. And you shall find my words as mighty wings to your faltering understanding.

Consider Nature all about you. Do you not find it built upon the ovum principle? Yea, in the ovum you shall find the key to all creation.

An ovum is your head, your heart, your eye. An ovum is every fruit and every seed thereof. An ovum is a drop of water and every sperm of every living creature. And the countless orbs tracing their mystic charts upon the face of heavens – are they not all ova containing the quintessence of Life – the *Micro*-God – in varying stages of unfolding? Is not all Life constantly hatching out of an ovum and going back into an ovum?

Miraculous, indeed, and continuous is the process of creation. The flow of Life from the surface of the Mother Ovum into the centre thereof, and from the centre unto the surface goes on uninterrupted. As he expands in Time and Space the *Micro*-God in the central nucleus passes from ovum to ovum, from the lowest to the highest order of Life, the lowest being the least and the highest the most expanded in Time and Space, and the time required for passage from one ovum into another varying from a twinkle in some cases to an æon in others. And so the process goes on until the shell of the Mother Ovum is pierced, and the *Micro*-God emerges as *Macro*-God.

Thus is Life an unfolding, a growth and a progress, but not as men are wont to speak of growth and progress. For growth to them is an accretion in bulk, and progress, a going forward. Whereas growth is an all around expansion in Time and Space, and progress is a motion extending equally in all directions: backward as well as forward, and downward and sideward as well as upward. The ultimate growth, therefore, is the outgrowing of Space; and the ultimate progress is the outstripping of Time, thus merging into *Macro*-God and reaching His freedom from bonds of Time and Space, which is the only freedom worth the name. And that is the destiny set for Man.

Ponder well these words, O monks. Except your very blood imbibe them with a relish, your efforts to free yourselves and others are apt to add more links to your chains and theirs. Mirdad would have you understand that you may help all yearners to understand.

Mirdad would have you free that you may lead to Freedom the race of those who long to overcome and to be free. Therefore would he elucidate still further this ovum principle, particularly in so far as it touches Man.

All orders of being below Man are enclosed in group ova. Thus there are for plants as many ova as there are varieties of plants, the more evolved enclosing all the less evolved. And so it is with insects, fishes and mammals; always the more evolved enclosing all the orders of Life below it down to the central nucleus.

As the yolk and white within the common egg serve to feed and evolve the embryo chick therein, so do all the ova enclosed in any ovum serve to feed and unfold the *Micro*-God therein.

In each successive ovum the *Micro*-God finds space-time food slightly different from that furnished him in the preceding ovum. Hence the difference in space-time expansion. Diffused and formless in the Gas, he becomes more concentrated and approaches form in the Liquid; while in the mineral he assumes a definite form and fixity remaining all the while devoid of any attributes of Life as manifested in the higher forms. In the Vegetable he takes on form with the capacity to grow, to multiply and to feel. In the Animal he feels, and moves, and propagates, has memory and rudiments of thought. But in Man, in addition to all that, he acquires a *personality* and the ability to *contemplate, to express himself* and *to create*. To be sure, Man's creation in comparison to God's is like a house of cards built by an infant compared to a glorious temple, or a graceful castle built by a super-architect. Yet is it creation none the less.

Each man becomes an *individual* ovum, the more evolved enclosing the less evolved plus all the animal vegetable and the lower ova down to the central nucleus. While the most evolved – the Overcomer – encloses all the human and the less than human ova.

The *size* of the ovum enclosing any man is *measured* by the breadth of the space-time horizons of that man. While one man's consciousness of Time embraces no more than the brief span from his infancy to the present hour, and his Space horizons encompass no more than his eye can reach, another's horizons encompass pasts immemorial and futures far in the distance, and leagues of spaces yet untraversed by his eye.

The food provided all men for their unfolding is the same; but their capacity of feeding and digesting is not the same; for they have not hatched out of the same ovum at the same time and place. Hence the difference in their space-time expansion; and hence no two can be found who are exactly alike.

From the same board, so richly and so lavishly spread before all men, one feasts on the purity and beauty of gold, and is filled; while another feasts upon the gold itself, and is ever hungry. A hunter, looking at a roe, is prompted to kill it and consume it. A poet, looking at the same roe, is carried as on wings into spaces and times of which the hunter never dreams. Micayon, living in the same Ark with Shamadam, dreams of ultimate freedom and the summit of release from the bounds of Time and Space; while Shamadam is ever busy hobbling himself with longer and sturdier hawsers of Space and Time. Verily, Micayon and Shamadam, though touching elbows, are far apart. Micayon contains Shamadam; but Shamadam contains not Micayon. Therefore can Micayon understand Shamadam, but Shamadam cannot understand Micayon.

An Overcomer's life touches the life of every man on every side; for it contains the lives of all men. Whereas no man's life touches an Overcomer's life on every side. To the simplest of men the Overcomer appears as the simplest of men. To the highly evolved he appears as one highly evolved. But there are always sides of him which no man less than an Overcomer can ever feel and understand. Hence his solitude and sense of being in the world yet not of it.

The *Micro*-God would not be confined. He is ever working for his own release from Time and Space confinement, using an intelligence far surpassing the human. In lower beings men call it *instinct*. In ordinary men they call it *reason*. In higher men they designate it as *prophetic sense*. It is all that and much more than that. It is that nameless power which some have aptly named The Holy Spirit, and which Mirdad names the Spirit of Holy Understanding.

The first Son of Man who pierced the shell of Time and crossed the bourn of Space is rightly called the Son of God. His understanding of his godhood is fitly called the Holy Spirit. But be assured that you also are sons of God, and in you also is The Holy Spirit working his way. Work with him and never against him.

But till you pierce the shell of Time and cross the bourn of Space let no one say 'I AM GOD'. Say, rather, 'GOD IS I'. This keep you well ın mind lest haughtiness and vain imaginings corrupt your hearts and militate against the Holy Spirit's work within you. For most men work against the Holy Spirit's work, and thus delay their ultimate release.

To conquer Time you must fight Time with Time. To vanquish Space you must let Space eat Space. To play the kindly host to either is to remain the prisoner of both, and the hostage to the endless antics of Good and Evil.

Those who have found their destiny and yearn to work it out lose no time coddling Time, and no steps pacing Space. In one short lifetime they may roll up æons and annihilate stupendous vasts. They do not wait on Death to take them into the ovum next to theirs; they trust to Life to help them pierce the shells of many ova all at once.

For that you must be dispossessed of everything, that Time and Space may have no hold upon your hearts. The more you possess, the more you are possessed. The less you possess, the less you are possessed.

Aye, be dispossessed of everything except your Faith, your Love, and your yearning for release through Holy Understanding.

# CHAPTER THIRTY-FIVE

# Sparks upon the Godward Path

MIRDAD: In the stillness of this night Mirdad would sprinkle a few sparks upon your Godward path:

Avoid disputes. Truth is an axiom; it needs no proof. Whatever must be propped with argument and proof is soon or late knocked down with proof and argument.

To prove a thing is to disprove its opposite. To prove its opposite is to disprove it. God has no opposites. How shall you *prove* or *disprove* Him?

To be a conduit for Truth the tongue must never be a flail, a fang, a weather-vane, an acrobat, or a scavenger.

Speak to relieve the speechless. Be speechless to relieve yourselves.

Words are vessels that ply the seas of Space and touch at many ports. Take care as to what you load them with; for having run their course, they shall ultimately discharge their cargo at your gate.

What the broom is to the house, self-searching is to the heart. Sweep well your hearts.

A well-swept heart is a fortress unassailable.

As you feed on men and things so they feed on you. Be wholesome food to others if you would not be poisoned.

When in doubt about the next step, stand still.

What you dislike dislikes you. Like it and let it be, thus removing an obstacle from your path.

The most unendurable nuisance is to consider anything a nuisance.

Take your choice: Either to own all things, or nothing at all. No middle course is possible.

Every stumbling-block is a warning. Read the warning well, and the stumbling-block shall become a beacon.

The straight is the brother of the crooked. The one is a short cut; the other, a roundabout way. Have patience with the crooked.

Patience is health when leaning upon Faith. When unaccompanied by Faith it is paralysis.

*To be, to feel, to think, to imagine, to know* – Behold the order of the main stages in the circuit of human life.

Beware of giving and receiving praise, even when most sincere and deserved. As to flattery, be deaf and dumb to its insidious vows.

You borrow everything you give so long as you are conscious of giving.

In truth you can give naught which is yours. You only give to men what you keep in trust for men. That which is yours – and yours alone – you cannot give away even if you desired.

Keep equipoised, and you shall be the standard and the scales for men to measure and to weigh themselves.

There is nor poverty nor riches. There is the knack of using things. The really poor is he who misuses what he has. The really rich is he who well uses what he has.

Even a mouldy crust of bread may be riches beyond computing. Even a cellar stocked with gold may be poverty beyond relief.

Where many roads converge do not hesitate as to which one to follow. To a God-seeking heart all roads lead to God.

Approach in reverence all forms of Life. In the least significant is hid the key to the most significant.

All works of Life are significant – yea marvellous, surpassing and inimitable, Life busies not itself with useless trifles.

To issue from the workshops of Nature a thing must be worthy of Nature's loving care and most painstaking art. Should it not be worthy of your respect, at least?

If gnats and ants be worthy of respect, how much more so your fellow-men?

Disdain no man. Better to be disdained by every man than to disdain a single man.

For to disdain a man is to disdain the *Micro*-God within him. to disdain the *Micro*-God in any man is to disdain Him in yourselves. How shall he ever reach his haven who scorns his only pilot to that haven?

Look up to see what is below. Look down to see what is above.

Descend as much as you ascend; else you lose your balance.

To-day you are disciples. To-morrow you shall be teachers. To be good teachers you must remain good disciples.

Seek not to weed out Evil from the world; for even weeds make good manure.

Zeal misapplied too often kills the zealot.

Tall and stately trees alone do not make up a forest. Some underbrush and clinging vine are always necessary.

Hypocrisy may be driven under cover – for a while; it cannot be kept there forever, nor can it be smoked out and exterminated.

Dark passions breed and prosper in the dark. Allow them the freedom of light if you would decrease their brood.

If out of a thousand hypocrites you succeed in reclaiming one to simple honesty, then great, indeed, is your success.

Set a beacon aloft and go not about calling men to see it. Those who are in need of light need no invitation to light.

Wisdom is a burden to the half-wise as is folly to the fool. Assist the half-wise with his burden and let the fool alone; the half-wise can teach him more than you can.

Often you shall think your road impassable, sombre and companionless. Have will and plod along; and round each curve you shall find a new companion.

No road in the trackless Space is yet untravelled. Where the footprints are few and far apart the road is safe and straight, though rough in spots and lonely.

Guides can show the way to those who would be shown; they cannot force them to walk it. Remember that you are guides.

To guide well one must be well guided. Depend upon your Guide.

Many shall say to you, 'Show us the way'. But few, too few, shall say, 'Lead us, we pray you, in the way'.

On the way to overcoming the few count more than the many.

Creep where you cannot walk. Walk where you cannot run. Run where you cannot fly. Fly where you cannot bring the whole universe to a standstill within you.

Not once, nor twice, nor yet a hundred times must you raise the man who stumbles while endeavouring to follow your lead. Keep raising him till he stumbles no more, remembering that you, too, once were babes.

Anoint your hearts and minds with forgiveness that you may dream anointed dreams.

Life is a fever of varying intensity and kinds, depending on each man's obsession; and men are ever in delirium. Blessed are they who are delirious of Holy Freedom which is the fruit of Holy Understanding.

Men's fevers are transmutable. The fever of war may be transmuted into a fever of peace. The fever of hoarding wealth, into a fever of hoarding love. Such is the alchemy of the Spirit which you are called upon to practise and to teach.

Preach Life to the dying, and to the living, Death. But to those who yearn to overcome preach deliverance from both.

Vast is the difference between 'holding' and 'being held'. You hold only what you love. What you hate holds you. Avoid being held.

More earths than one are spinning their courses across the voids of Time and Space. Yours is the youngest of the family, and a very lusty babe she is.

A still motion – what a paradox! Yet that is the motion of the worlds in God.

Look at the fingers on your hands if you would know how unequal things can be equal.

Chance is the plaything of the wise. Fools are the playthings of Chance.

Never complain of anything. To complain of a thing is to make of it a scourge for the complainer. To endure it well is to scourge it well. But to understand it is to make of it a faithful servant.

It often happens that a hunter aiming, say, at a roe would miss the roe and kill a hare of whose presence he was entirely unaware. A wise hunter will say in such a case, 'It was really the hare I had aimed at, and not the roe. And I got my quarry.'

Aim well, and any result is a good result.

What comes to you is yours. What delays in coming is not worth waiting for. Let it do the waiting.

You never miss an aim, if what you aim at aims at you.

An aim missed is always an aim attained. Let your hearts be Disappointment-proof.

Disappointment is a kite hatched out by flabby hearts and brought up on the carrions of their hopes miscarried.

A hope fulfilled becomes the mother of many stillborn hopes. Beware of giving your hearts in marriage unto Hope if you would not convert them into graveyards.

One out of a hundred eggs spawned by a fish may come to fruition. Yet are the ninety-nine not wasted. So prodigal and so discriminately indiscriminate is Nature. Be you likewise prodigal and discriminately indiscriminate in sowing your hearts and minds in the hearts and minds of men.

Seek no reward for any labour done. The labour itself is reward sufficient to the labourer who loves his labour.

Remember the Creative Word and the Perfect Balance. When you have reached that Balance through Holy Understanding, then only shall you have become overcomers, and then shall your hands collaborate with the hands of God.

May the peace and stillness of this night vibrate in you until you drown them in the stillness and the peace of Holy Understanding.

So taught I Noah.

So I teach you.

# CHAPTER THIRTY-SIX

## Day of the Ark and its Rituals.
## The Message from the Prince of Bethar
## about the Living Lamp

*Naronda*: Since the Master's return from Bethar Shamadam had been sulky and retiring. But as the Day of the Ark approached he became high-spirited and vivacious and took a personal command of all the intricate preparations down to the minutest detail.

Like the Day of the Vine, the Day of the Ark had been stretched from a single day unto a whole week of lively festivities and brisk trading in all sorts of goods and chattels.

Of the many rituals peculiar to this Day the most important are: the slaughtering of a bullock to be offered in sacrifice, the kindling of the sacrificial fire, and the lighting from that fire of the new lamp which is to take the place of the old one on the altar; all of which is carried on by the Senior with much ceremony, the public assisting and ending by each lighting a candle from the new lamp, which candles are later extinguished and jealously kept as talismans against evil spirits. At the end of the ceremonies it is customary for the Senior to deliver an oration.

The pilgrims to the Day of the Ark, like those to the Day of the Vine, rarely come without some gifts and donations of one kind or another. The majority, however, bring bullocks, rams and he-goats, ostensibly to be sacrificed with the bullock offered by the Ark, but in reality to be added to the Ark's livestock, but not slaughtered.

The new lamp is usually presented by some prince or magnate of the Milky Mountains. And since it is considered a great honour and a privilege to make the present, and since the contenders are many, the custom was established to settle the choice for each year by lots drawn at the close of the preceding year's festivities. The princes and the magnates vie in zeal and in devotion, each aiming that his lamp should outshine all its predecessors in costliness and beauty of design and craftsmanship.

The lot for this year's lamp was drawn by the prince of Bethar. And all waited to behold the new treasure; for the prince was famed for his open-handed wealth as well as for his fervour towards the Ark.

On the eve of that day Shamadam called us and the Master into his cell and spoke to us as follows, addressing more the Master than the rest:

*Shamadam*: To-morrow is an holy day; and it behooves us all to keep it holy.

Whatever be the quarrels of the past let us inter them here and now. The Ark must not be made to slack its forward pace, or to abate its ardour. And God forbid it should be made to halt.

I am the Senior of this Ark. Mine is the onerous duty of commanding. Mine is the vested right to lay the course. The duty and the right fell to me by succession, as they shall surely fall to one of you when I am dead and gone. As I bided my time bide you your time.

If I have wronged Mirdad, let him forgive my wrong.

MIRDAD: You have not wronged Mirdad; but you have wronged Shamadam very grievously.

*Shamadam*: Is not Shamadam free to wrong Shamadam?

MIRDAD: Free to do wrong? How most incongruous the very words! For to do wrong even to one's own self is to become a bondsman to one's wrong. While to do wrong to others is to become a bondsman's bondsman. Ah, heavy is the weight of wrong.

*Shamadam*: If I be willing to support my wrong, what is that to you?

MIRDAD: Shall a diseased tooth say to the mouth, What is my pain to you if I be willing to endure it?

*Shamadam*: Ah, let me be, just let me be. Turn your heavy hand away from me, and flail me not with your clever tongue. Let me live out the balance of my days as I have lived and laboured hitherto. Go build your ark elsewhere, but leave this Ark alone. The world is wide for you and me and for your ark and mine. To-morrow is *my* day. Stand you aside and let me do my work; for I shall brook no interference on the part of anyone of you.

Take care. Shamadam's vengeance is as terrible as God's. Take care. Take care.

*Naronda*: When we went out of the Senior's cell the Master gently shook his head and said:

MIRDAD: Shamadam's heart is still Shamadam's heart.

*Naronda*: On the morrow, much to Shamadam's delight, the ceremonies were carried out punctiliously and without untoward incidents up to the moment when the new lamp was to be presented and lighted.

At that moment a very tall and stately man, dressed in white, was seen elbowing his way with difficulty through the dense crowd and heading towards the altar. On the instant the whisper went from mouth to mouth that the man was the personal emissary of the prince of Bethar carrying the new lamp; and all were anxious to lay eyes upon the precious treasure.

Shamadam bowed very low to the messenger believing, like the rest, that he carried the priceless gift for the new year. But the man, having said something at low breath to Shamadam, drew a parchment out of his pocket and, after explaining that it was a message from the prince of Bethar which he was charged to deliver in person, began to read:

'From the erstwhile prince of Bethar to all his fellow-men of the Milky Mountains assembled on this day in the Ark – peace and brotherly love.

'Of my fervid devotion to the Ark you are all living witnesses. As the honour of presenting the lamp for this year fell to my lot I spared not wit nor wealth in order that my gift be worthy of the Ark. And well were my efforts rewarded. For the lamp that my wealth and my craftsmen's cunning had finally wrought out was verily a marvel to behold.

'But God was forbearing and kind, and would not expose my wretched poverty. For he has led me since unto a lamp whose light is dazzling and inextinguishable, whose beauty is surpassing and untarnishing. Having beheld that lamp I became full of shame for having ever thought my lamp of any value whatsoever. So I consigned it to the rubbish heap.

'It is that living lamp, not wrought with hands, which I most earnestly commend to all of you. Upon it feast your eyes, and from it light your candles. Behold, it is within your reach. The name of it is MIRDAD.

'May you be worthy of his light.'

Scarcely had the messenger uttered the last words when Shamadam, who had been standing by his side, suddenly vanished as if he were a ghost. The Master's name went through the huge assembly like a gust of mighty wind through a virgin forest. All wished to see the living lamp of whom the prince of Bethar spoke so enticingly in his message.

Presently the Master was seen to mount the steps of the altar and to face the crowd. And instantly the heaving human mass became a single man, attentive, eager and alert. Then the Master spoke, and said,

# CHAPTER THIRTY-SEVEN

# The Master warns the Crowds
of the Flood of Fire and Blood,
Points the Way of Escape,
and Launches his Ark

MIRDAD: What seek you of Mirdad? A golden jewelled lamp to decorate the altar? But neither is Mirdad a goldsmith, nor a jeweller, albeit he be a lighthouse and a haven.

Or seek you talismans to ward off evil eyes? Aye, talismans in plenty has Mirdad, but of another kind.

Or seek you light that you may safely walk each in his appointed path? How very strange, indeed! Have you the sun, the moon, the stars, yet fear to stumble and to fall? Then were your eyes unfit to serve as guides; else were the light too scanty for the eyes. And who of you would do without his eyes? Who would accuse the sun of being niggardly?

Of what avail the eye that keeps the foot from stumbling on its path, but leaves the heart to stumble and to bleed as it gropes vainly for a path?

Of what avail the light that overfills the eye, yet leaves the spirit void and unillumined?

What seek you of Mirdad? If it be seeing hearts, and spirits bathed in light that you desire and clamour for, then verily you clamour not in vain. For my concern is with the spirit and the heart of Man.

What brought you as an offering unto this Day, which is a day of glorious overcoming? Brought you he-goats, and rams and bullocks? How very cheap the price you would pay for deliverance! Rather how very cheap is the deliverance you would buy.

It were no glory for a man to overcome a goat. And verily is it a great disgrace for any man to offer up a poor goat's life in ransom for his own.

What have you done to share in the spirit of this Day, which is a day of Faith unfurled and Love supremely justified?

Aye, to be sure, you have performed a multiplicity of rites, and mumbled many prayers. But doubt accompanied your every move and hatred said 'Amen' to every prayer.

Are you not here to celebrate the conquest of the Flood? How come you celebrate a victory which left you vanquished? For in subduing his own deeps Noah subdued not your deeps, but only pointed out the way. And, lo your deeps are full of rage and threaten to shipwreck you. Ere you have overcome your flood, you are not worthy of this Day.

Each of you is a flood, an ark and a commander. And till you reach the day when you can disembark unto a freshly washed and virgin earth be not in haste to celebrate the victory.

You would know how it came about that Man became a flood unto himself.

When Holy Omniwill clove Adam into twain that he may know himself and realize his oneness with the One, then he became a *male* and a *female* – an he-Adam and a she-Adam. Then was he deluged with desires which are the offspring of Duality – desires so numerous, so infinite of hues, so very great of magnitude, so profligate and so prolific that till this day Man is a derelict upon their waves. No sooner does a wave lift him to dizzy heights than does another drag him to the bottom. For his desires are paired as he himself is paired. And though two opposites but complement each other in reality, yet to the ignorant they seem at grips and blows and never willing to declare even a moment's truce.

That is the flood that Man is called to breast hour by hour, day by day, throughout his very long and arduous dual life.

That is the flood whose mighty fountains gush out of the heart and sweep you in their rush.

That is the flood whose rainbow shall not grace your sky until your sky be wedded to your earth and made with it as one.

Since Adam sowed himself in Eve men have been reaping whirlwinds and floods. When passions of a kind preponderate, then is the life of men thrown out of balance, and then are men engulfed in one flood or another in order that a balance be established. And never shall the balance be adjusted till men have learned to knead all their desires in the kneading trough of Love and bake of them the bread of Holy Understanding.

The flood that overwhelmed the Earth in Noah's days was not

the first nor last humanity has known. It only set a high mark in the long succession of devastating floods. The flood of fire and blood which is about to break upon the Earth shall surely pass the mark. Are you prepared to float, or shall you be submerged?

Alas! You are too busy adding weight on weight; too busy drugging your blood with pleasures rife with pain; too busy charting roads that lead you to nowhere; too busy picking seed in the backyards of the storerooms of Life without so much as peeping through the keyhole. How shall you not go under, O my waifs?

You, born to soar aloft, to roam the boundless space, to fold the universe within your wings, have cooped yourselves in coops of snug conventions and beliefs that clip your wings, impair your sight and petrify your sinews. How shall you override the coming flood, my waifs?

You, images and likenesses of God, have well-nigh blotted out the likeness and the image. Your godly stature have you dwarfed till you no longer recognize it. Your countenance divine have you besmeared with mud, and masked with many clownish masks. How shall you face the flood you have unleashed, my waifs?

Except you heed Mirdad, the Earth shall never be to you more than a tomb, the Sky more than a shroud. Whereas the one was fitted out to serve you for a cradle, the other, for a throne.

Again I say to you, You are the flood, the ark and the commander. Your passions are the flood. Your body is the ark. Your faith is the commander. But penetrating all is your will. And hovering over all is your understanding.

Make certain that the ark be stanch and seaworthy; but do not waste your life on that alone; else will the time for sailing never come, and in the end both you and your ark will rot and be submerged upon the spot. Make certain of the captain's competence and calm. But above all learn to seek out the sources of the flood, and train your will to dry them one by one. Then surely will the flood abate and finally spend itself.

Burn out a passion ere it burns you out.

Look not into a passion's mouth to see if it have fangs or honeyed mandibles. The bee that gathers up the nectar of the flowers gathers their poison, too.

Nor scrutinize a passion's face if it be comely or unsightly.

More comely was to Eve the Serpent's face than was the face of God.

Nor put a passion in the scales to ascertain its weight. Who would compare in weight a diadem with a mountain? Yet, verily, the diadem is heavier by far than the mountain.

And there be passions that carol celestial lays by day, but hiss and bite and sting under the pall of night; and passions fat and over-weighed with joy that quickly turn to skeletons of sorrow; and passions soft of eye and docile of demeanour that suddenly become more ravenous than wolves, more treacherous than hyenas; and passions scenting sweeter than a rose so long as left alone, but stinking worse than carrions and skunks so soon as touched and plucked.

Sift not your passions into good and bad, for that is labour lost. The good cannot endure without the bad; the bad can strike no roots save in the good.

One is the tree of Good and Evil. One is the fruit thereof. You cannot know the taste of Good without at once knowing the taste of Evil.

The pap from which you suck the milk of Life the same it is that yields the milk of Death. The hand that rocks you in the cradle is but the very hand that digs your grave.

That is, my waifs, the nature of Duality. Be not so vain and obstinate as to attempt to change it. Be not so foolish as to try to split it into halves that you may take the half you like and cast the other out.

Would you be masters of Duality? Treat it as neither good nor evil.

Has not the milk of life and death turned sour in your mouths? Is it not time you rinsed your mouths with something that is neither good nor bad because surpassing both? Is it not time you yearned for the fruit which is nor sweet nor bitter because not grown upon the tree of Good and Evil?

Would you be free from the clutches of Duality? Then pluck its tree – the tree of Good and Evil – out of your hearts. Aye, pluck it root and branch that the seed of Life Divine, the seed of Holy Understanding which is beyond all good and evil, may germinate and sprout instead thereof.

A cheerless message is Mirdad's you say. It robs us of the joy of waiting on the morrow. It makes us dumb, disinterested witnesses in life, when we would be vociferous contestants. For sweet is it to contest no matter what the stakes at issue. And sweet to venture on a chase even though the quarry be nothing more than a will-o'-the-wisp.

So say you in your hearts, forgetting that your hearts are not yours at all so long as good and evil passions hold their reins.

To be the masters of your hearts knead all your passions – good and bad – in the single trough of Love that you may bake them in the oven of Holy Understanding where all duality is unified in God.

Cease now to trouble a world already overtroubled.

How do you hope to draw clean water from a well wherein you dump incessantly all kinds of rubbish and of mud? How shall the waters in a pool ever be clear and still if you disturb them every moment?

Draw no drafts for calm upon a troubled world lest you be drawing drafts on Trouble.

Draw no drafts for love upon a hating world lest you be drawing drafts on Hate.

Draw no drafts for life upon a dying world lest you be drawing drafts on Death. The world can pay you in no other coin except its own which is a two-faced coin.

But draw drafts on your infinite God-self which is so rich in peaceful Understanding.

Make no demands upon the world which you make not upon yourselves. Nor make demands on any man which you allow him not to make on you.

And what is that which, if accorded you by all the world, would help you overcome your flood and disembark upon an earth divorced from pain and death and joined to heaven in everlasting Love and peace of Understanding? Is it possessions, power, fame? Is it authority, and prestige and respect? Is it ambition crowned, and hope fulfilled? But each of these is but a fountainhead which nourishes your flood. Away with them, my waifs, away, away.

Be still that you may be clear.

Be clear that you may clearly see the world.

When you see clearly through the world, then will you know how very poor and powerless it is to give you what you seek of freedom, peace and life.

All that the world can give you is a body – an ark in which to sail the sea of dual life. And that you owe to no man in the world. The universe is duty-bound to furnish it to you and to sustain it. To keep it trim and stanch to breast the flood, as trim and stanch was Noah's ark; to leash the beasts therein and have them well controlled, as Noah leashed his beasts and perfectly controlled them – that is your duty, and yours alone.

To have a faith bright-eyed and wide-awake which to put at the helm; a faith unshaken in the Omniwill which is your guide to Eden's blissful portals – that is your business, and yours alone.

To have a dauntless will for a commander; a will to overcome and to partake of Holy Understanding's Tree of Life – that is again your work, and yours alone.

God-bound is Man. No destination short of that is worthy of his pain. What if the way be long and strewn with squalls and gales? Shall not pure-hearted, keen-eyed Faith outwit the squall and override the gale?

Make haste. For time bestowed on loitering is pain-infested time. And men, even the busiest, are loiterers, indeed.

Shipbuilders are you all. And sailors are you all. That is the task assigned you from eternity that you may sail the boundless ocean which is you and therein find that voiceless harmony of being whose name is God.

All things must have a centre from which to radiate and round which to revolve.

If life – Man's life – be a circle, and God-finding be thereof the centre, then all your work must be concentric with that centre; else were it loitering, though it be drenched in crimson perspiration.

But since to lead Man to his destiny is the business of Mirdad, behold! Mirdad has fitted out for you a wondrous ark, an ark well built and well commanded. Not one of gopher wood and pitch; nor one for ravens, lizards and hyenas. But one of Holy Understanding which shall indeed be a beacon for all who yearn to overcome. Her ballast shall not be wine-jars and presses, but hearts abrim with love for everything and all. Nor shall her cargo be lands and chattels, or silver, gold and jewels, but souls divorced from their shadows and mantled in the light and freedom of Understanding.

Let those who would break their moorings from the Earth; and those who would be unified; and those who yearn to overcome themselves – let them come aboard.

The Ark is ready.

The wind is favouring.

The sea is calm.

So taught I Noah.

So I teach you.

*Naronda*: When the Master stopped, a rustling went through the hitherto motionless assembly as if they had held their breath throughout the Master's words.

Before descending from the altar steps the Master called for the Seven and the harp, and with their aid began to sing the hymn of the New Ark. The crowd caught up the melody, and like a mighty wave swelled heavenward the sweet refrain,

*God is your captain, sail, my Ark!*


*Here ends that portion of the*
*Book which is permitted me*
*to publish to the world.*
*As for the rest,*
*its hour is*
*not yet.*
*M.N.*

PENGUIN

ARKANA

# NEW AGE BOOKS FOR MIND, BODY & SPIRIT

With over 200 titles currently in print, Arkana is the leading name in quality books for mind, body and spirit. Arkana encompasses the spirituality of both East and West, ancient and new. A vast range of interests is covered, including Psychology and Transformation, Health, Science and Mysticism, Women's Spirituality, Zen, Western Traditions and Astrology.

If you would like a catalogue of Arkana books, please write to:

Sales Dept. – Arkana
Penguin  Books USA Inc.
375 Hudson Street
New York, NY 10014

Arkana Marketing Department
Penguin Books Ltd
27 Wrights Lane
London W8 5TZ

PENGUIN

ARKANA

# NEW AGE BOOKS FOR MIND, BODY & SPIRIT

## A SELECTION OF TITLES

### Weavers of Wisdom: Women Mystics of the Twentieth Century
Anne Bancroft

Throughout history women have sought answers to eternal questions about existence and beyond – yet most gurus, philosophers and religious leaders have been men. Through exploring the teachings of fifteen women mystics – each with her own approach to what she calls 'the truth that goes beyond the ordinary' – Anne Bancroft gives a rare, cohesive and fascinating insight into the diversity of female approaches to mysticism.

### Dynamics of the Unconscious: Seminars in Psychological Astrology II
Liz Greene and Howard Sasportas

The authors of The *Development of the Personality* team up again to show how the dynamics of depth psychology interact with your birth chart. They shed new light on the psychology and astrology of aggression and depression – the darker elements of the adult personality that we must confront if we are to grow to find the wisdom within.

### The Myth of the Eternal Return: Cosmos and History   Mircea Eliade

'A luminous, profound, and extremely stimulating work … Eliade's thesis is that ancient man envisaged events not as constituting a linear, progressive history, but simply as so many creative repetitions of primordial archetypes … This is an essay which everyone interested in the history of religion and in the mentality of ancient man will have to read. It is difficult to speak too highly of it' – Theodore H. Gaster in *Review of Religion*

### The Second Krishnamurti Reader   Edited by Mary Lutyens

In this reader bringing together two of Krishnamurti's most popular works, *The Only Revolution* and *The Urgency of Change*, the spiritual teacher who rebelled against religion points to a new order arising when we have ceased to be envious and vicious. Krishnamurti says, simply: 'When you are not, love is.' 'Seeing,' he declares, 'is the greatest of all skills.' In these pages, gently, he helps us to open our hearts and eyes.

PENGUIN

ARKANA

# NEW AGE BOOKS FOR MIND, BODY & SPIRIT

## A SELECTION OF TITLES

### When the Iron Eagle Flies: Buddhism for the West   Ayya Khema

'One of humanity's greatest jewels'. Such are the teachings of the Buddha, unfolded here simply, free of jargon. This practical guide to meaning through awareness contains a wealth of exercises and advice to help the reader on his or her way.

### The Second Ring of Power   Carlos Casteneda

Carlos Castaneda's journey into the world of sorcery has captivated millions. In this fifth book, he introduces the reader to Dona Soledad, whose mission is to test Castaneda by a series of terrifying tricks. Thus Castaneda is initiated into experiences so intense, so profoundly disturbing, as to be an assault on reason and on every preconceived notion of life...

### Dialogues with Scientists and Sages: The Search for Unity
Renée Weber

In their own words, contemporary scientists and mystics – from the Dalai Lama to Stephen Hawking – share with us their richly diverse views on space, time, matter, energy, life, consciousness, creation and our place in the scheme of things. Through the immediacy of verbatim dialogue, we encounter scientists who endorse mysticism, and those who oppose it; mystics who dismiss science, and those who embrace it.

### The Way of the Sufi   Idries Shah

Sufism, the mystical aspect of Islam, has had a dynamic and lasting effect on the literature of that religion. Its teachings, often elusive and subtle, aim at the perfecting and completing of the human mind. In this wide-ranging anthology of Sufi writing Idries Shah offers a broad selection of poetry, contemplations, letters, lectures and teaching stories that together form an illuminating introduction to this unique body of thought.

PENGUIN

ARKANA

# NEW AGE BOOKS FOR MIND, BODY & SPIRIT

## A SELECTION OF TITLES

**Meeting Life**  Krishnamurti

In the last teachings before his death in 1986, Kirshnamurti suggests that we  solve our problems most effectively when we let go of everything we know and purport to be, and meditate – which entails no more than dropping our hurts, fears, anxiety, loneliness, despair and sorrow on the spot. 'That is the foundation, that is the first step, and the first step,' he insists, 'is the last step.'

**GAIA: The Growth of an Idea**  Lawrence E. Joseph

Many cultures use the figure of Mother Earth to express the idea that the Earth is a *living creature*; with the Gaia Hypothesis, the idea has now attained the status of science. In this immensely readable book the author describes how James E. Lovelock came to formulate the hypothesis, how it was developed and how it has subsequently been acclaimed and argued over by an international array of scientists.

**Tertium Organum**  P. D. Ouspensky

First published in 1912, *Tertium Organum* was the first major work to re-examine the ancient and still largely unresolved philosophical problem of the nature of consciousness. In it Ouspensky conducts a fascinating post-Kantian inquiry into many of the major issues that have preoccupied generations of Western philosophers – an inquiry that bridges the gulf between Wetern rationalism and Eastern mysticism.

**Saturn: A New Look at an Old Devil**  Liz Greene

Liz Greene draws on the depth psychology of Jung to go beyond the simplistic view that we are controlled by our stars. The way Saturn moves through the different houses, she suggests, can reveal much about a person's conscious and unconscious impulses; but it is up to us to travel along the roads to fulfilment the Initiator planet offers. 'As deep and thorough as Saturn himself' – Cherry Gilchrist

PENGUIN

ARKANA

# NEW AGE BOOKS FOR MIND, BODY & SPIRIT

## A SELECTION OF TITLES

**A Course in Miracles**
The Course, Workbook for Students and Manual for Teachers

Hailed as 'one of the most remarkable systems of spiritual truth available today', *A Course in Miracles* is a self-study course designed to shift our perceptions, heal our minds and change our behaviour, teaching us to experience miracles – 'natural expressions of love' – rather than problems generated by fear in our lives.

**Fire in the Heart**  Kyriacos C. Markides

A sequel to *The Magus of Strovolus* and *Homage to the Sun*, *Fire in the Heart* centres on Daskalos, the Cypriot healer and miracle-worker and his successor-designate Kostas. The author, who has witnessed much that is startling in his years with the two magi, believes humanity may today be on the verge of a revolution in consciousness 'more profound than the Renaissance and the Enlightenment combined.'

**Arthur and the Sovereignty of Britain: Goddess and Tradition on the Mabinogion**  Caitlín Matthews

Rich in legend and the primitive magic of the Celtic Otherworld, the stories of the *Mabinogion* heralded the first flowering of European literature and became the source of Arthurian legend. Caitlín Matthews illuminates these stories, shedding light on Sovereignty, the Goddess of the Land and the spiritual principle of the Feminine.

**Shamanism: Archaic Techniques of Ecstasy**  Mircea Eliade

Throughout Siberia and Central Asia, religious life traditionally centres around the figure of the shaman: magician and medicine man, healer and miracle-doer, priest and poet. 'Has become the standard work on the subject and justifies its claim to be the first book to study the phenomenon over a wide field and in a properly religious context' – *The Times Literary Supplement*